# MODERN
# CONSTRUCTION
# PROJECT
# MANAGEMENT

# MODERN CONSTRUCTION PROJECT MANAGEMENT

## Second Edition

S.L. Tang
S.W. Poon
Syed M. Ahmed
Francis K.W. Wong

香港大學出版社
HONG KONG UNIVERSITY PRESS

**Hong Kong University Press**
14/F Hing Wai Centre
7 Tin Wan Praya Road
Aberdeen
Hong Kong

© Hong Kong University Press 2003

ISBN 962 209 567 4

British Library Cataloguing-in-Publication Data
A catalogue record for this book is available from the British Library.

Secure On-line Ordering
http://www.hkupress.org

Printed and bound by ColorPrint Production Ltd. in Hong Kong, China

# CONTENTS

Preface                                                                    vii

**Part I      Qualitative Project Management                      1**

1.    Principles of Organizational Structures                              3

2.    Organizational Structures for Contractors and Consultants           11

3.    Construction Contract I                                             23

4.    Construction Contract II                                            37

5.    Estimating and Tendering                                           47

6.    Resource Management and Planning                                   69

7.    Quality Management                                                 83

8.    Safety Management                                                  103

9.    Site Administration and Control                                    121

**Part II    Quantitative Project Management                    143**

10.    Network Diagram                                        145

11.    Critical Path Method                                   157

12.    Precedence Network                                     169

13.    PERT and Its Probability Concept                       181

14.    Time-Cost Optimization of a Project                    189

15.    Critical Path and Linear Programming                   199

16.    Contractual Claims Using CPM                           207

17.    Resource Management                                    215

18.    Common Programming Software                            227


Bibliography                                                  231

About the Authors                                             235

# PREFACE

This is a textbook written for undergraduates, postgraduate students and students of sub-professional technical courses in building and construction. It consists of simplified treatment of complex topics in construction project management, and the contents are biased towards Hong Kong practice. A substantial volume of data and information related to the Hong Kong construction industry has been collected, incorporated into existing knowledge, and methodically presented. Apart from students, many practising professionals and sub-professionals will also find the book useful.

The book is designed as a practical project management tool kit for the construction industry. It provides both the theories and the practical guidelines for every step of construction project management operations, and is written in simple and easy to understand English. The book is divided into two parts: qualitative project management (Part I) and quantitative project management (Part II). Part I includes the principles of organizational structures, organizational structures for contractors and consultants, construction contracts, estimating and tendering, resource management and planning, quality management, safety management, and site administration and control. Part II includes critical path network diagram formulation, analysis of critical path networks, precedence networks, PERT and its probability concept, time-cost optimization, linear programming techniques applied in critical path networks, contractual claim with the use of critical path analysis, resource histograms and resource allocation exercise, and finally an introduction to common computer packages for application in quantitative construction project management.

# PART I

# QUALITATIVE PROJECT MANAGEMENT

# 1

# PRINCIPLES OF ORGANIZATIONAL STRUCTURES

## 1. Introduction

An organizational structure involves a group of people among whom there are interaction, communication and coordination. There is usually an objective which the organization aims to achieve under a set of constraints. For example, a contractor's site organization has the objective of completing the works assigned to him, and the constraints are raw material supplies, labour supplies, finance and so on.

There are three principal types of organizational structures:
1. project organization
2. functional organization
3. matrix organization

## 2. Project Organization

In a project organization, each member of the team is responsible for a particular task. It is therefore task-oriented. An example of project organization is a highway project (Fig. 1.1) which consists of tunnelling, building and road works.

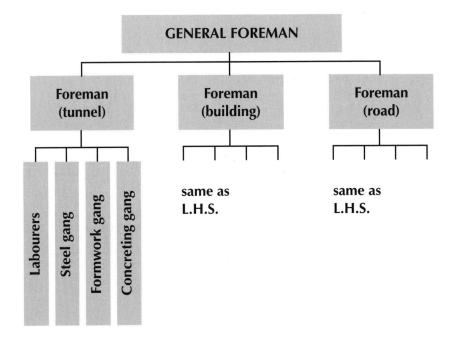

**Fig. 1.1**   Example of a project organization.

This form of organization has the merit of simplicity — each person is clearly instructed in his duty and authority. The disadvantage is that it sometimes does not fully utilize the resources available for each task.  For example, the concreting gang attached to the tunnel section does not work in the building section even thought it is idle at times. The merits and demerits of a project organization will be further discussed in section 4 of this chapter.

## 3.    Functional Organization

In contrast to the project organization (which is task-oriented), a functional organization is specialist-oriented. Specialists in each field are responsible for their own functions. An example of functional organization is shown in Fig.1.2.

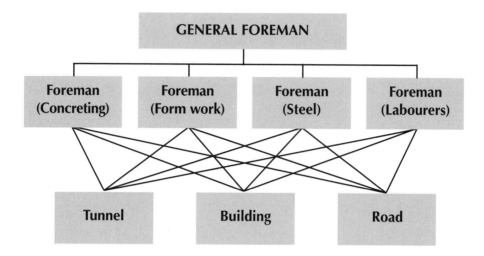

**Fig. 1.2**   Example of a functional organization.

From the organization chart (Fig 1.2), one can see that each foreman is responsible for carrying out work within his own specialism, e.g. for concrete work, steel work and so on. Each specialist contributes to the construction of tunnel, building and road works.

## 4.    Advantages and Disadvantages of Project Organization and Functional Organization

**4.1**    A comparison of the characteristics of the two forms of organizations is shown in Table 1.1.

| Characteristics | |
|---|---|
| **Project organization** | **Functional organization** |
| ♦ Branch heads are generalists. | ♦ Branch heads are specialists. |
| ♦ Suitable for works which must be completed in a specific time. | ♦ Suitable for works which run from calendar year to calendar year. |
| ♦ Suitable for dynamic works. | ♦ Suitable for routine works. |
| ♦ Suitable for relatively small organizations. | ♦ Suitable for large organizations. |

**Table 1.1**   Comparison of characteristics of project organization and functional organization.

**4.2**    There are some aspects in which the project organization is better than the functional organization. They are shown in Table 1.2.

| Advantages of project organization over functional organization | |
| --- | --- |
| **Project organization** | **Functional organization** |
| ◆ Fast decision, due to simple and clear lines of duty and responsibility. | ◆ Bureaucratic, probably due to protectionism between specialist branches. |
| ◆ More innovative, since problems are usually solved on the spot or within a branch. | ◆ Less innovative, since functions are separate and problems must be referred to the relevant branches. |
| ◆ Very efficient in achieving specific target. | ◆ Less efficient in achieving target. |

**Table 1.2**   Aspects in which project organization is more advantageous than functional organization.

**4.3**   There are also aspects in which the functional organization is better than the project organization. They are shown in Table 1.3.

| Advantages of functional organization over project organization | |
| --- | --- |
| **Project organization** | **Functional organization** |
| ◆ More expensive, because resources are sometimes not fully utilized. | ◆ Less expensive, because there is less wastage in utilizing resources. |
| ◆ Less chance for staff development on special knowledge or skill. | ◆ More chances for developing special knowledge or skill. |

**Table 1.3**   Aspects in which functional organization is more advantageous than project organization.

## 5.    Matrix Organization

A matrix organization is a combination of project organization and functional organization. Fig.1.3 shows an example of a matrix organization. One can see that the labourer foreman (functional) is at the same level as the other project foremen.

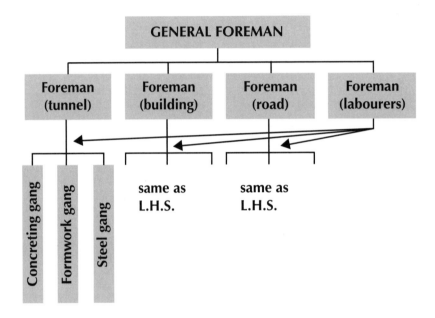

**Fig. 1.3**   Example of a matrix organization.

In this case, the project foremen do not have their own labourers. All labourers are supplied by a functional foreman who is at the same level/rank as the project foremen.

Sometimes, an organization can be purely matrix. Fig.1.4 shows an example of a purely matrix organization. In this purely-matrix organization, the project foremen do not have working gangs of their own. All resources are supplied by the functional foremen.

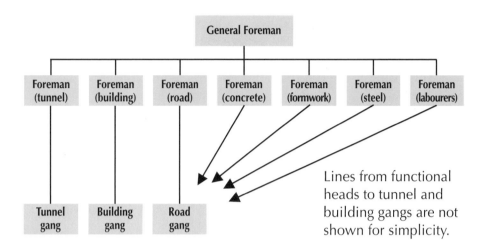

**Fig. 1.4**   Example of a purely matrix organization.

The purely matrix organization shown in Fig.1.4 is usually represented by a diagram which looks like a matrix (Fig.1.5). The horizontal lines represent functional responsibilities and the vertical lines represent project responsibilities.

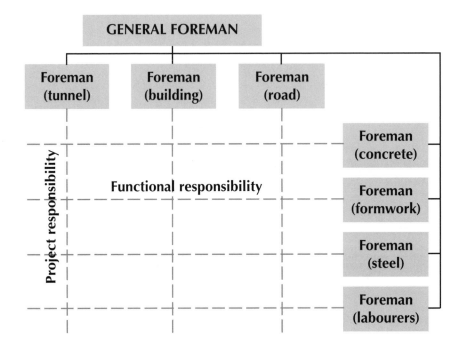

**Fig. 1.5** A typical matrix organization.

The matrix organization has the advantages of both the project and the functional organizations. It attempts to optimize the efficiency of an organization in a particular environment and for a particular objective. However, there is a disadvantage in a matrix organization: one person may work under two bosses. For example, a carpenter working under the formwork foreman, a functional foreman, will also be working under the road foreman, a project foreman (Fig.1.4). This is acceptable if the relationship between the formwork foreman and the road foreman is good, otherwise a lot of disputes may arise. Of course, the organization chart shows only the formal relationships; valuable informal relationships cannot be seen from the chart. These can increase cooperation within the organization, provided that the formal relationships are not overlooked.

In the next chapter, we will see how these different forms of organizations are applied in contracting and consulting firms.

# 2

# ORGANIZATIONAL STRUCTURES FOR CONTRACTORS AND CONSULTANTS

## 1. Introduction

This chapter will describe typical organization structures for contractors and consultants in Hong Kong. The organization structures drawn were all derived from real situations after surveying a considerable number of large contractors and consultants. First, the typical organization structure for a large contracting firm's head office will be discussed. Then that of a large consulting firm's head office will be described. A typical contractor's site organization structure will also be presented. Finally, the typical organization of a consultant's site representative, i.e. the resident engineer, will also be discussed.

## 2. Organization of a Contractor's Head Office

**2.1** Six large contracting firms' head office organizations in Hong Kong were surveyed. A typical organization structure was derived and is shown in Fig. 2.1. One can see that it is mainly a matrix organization (section 5 of Chapter 1). Each contracts manager undertakes several projects. Contracts managers are head office based. Under the contracts managers are project managers and site agents who are site based personnel (section 3 of this chapter).

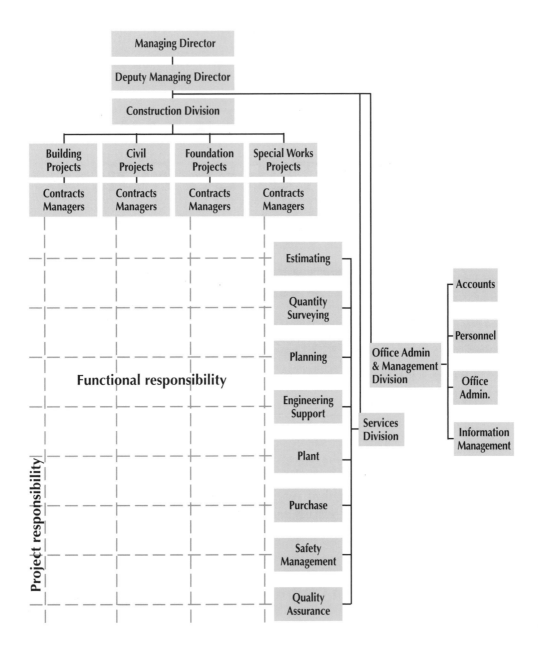

**Fig. 2.1**   A typical large contractor's head office organization.

**2.2**    **The estimating department** is responsible for preparing tenders for the company. It has to price a **bill of quantities** listed in the tender document. When pricing an item of work, it is necessary to consider the constituent parts (i.e. labour, plant, materials and overheads) in the estimation. It is also necessary to determine the parts of work that needed to be subcontracted. Assistance is usually required from the planning department to prepare a preliminary work programme and method statements for submission with the tender (section 2.4). In addition, assistance is needed from the purchase department for obtaining quotations of material supply and subcontracting work (section 2.7). After all items have been priced, the estimates will be forwarded to the company's top management who will add a profit mark-up.

**2.3**    The **quantity surveying department** is responsible for the assessment of work done and the subsequent payments of projects. It is also responsible for variations orders, subcontractor payments and claims for extra work. Another important duty of the department is the requisition of materials to be used in the project; in this respect it has to coordinate with the purchase department (section 2.7). Moreover, the department has to analyse the cash flow associated with the project so that the contractor is aware of his financial requirements. Usually, many of the quantity surveyors in this department are not attached to the head office but are placed on site (Fig. 2.2). The department is quite a big one in terms of the total number of staff. However, a small number of staff is required at the head office to coordinate site-based staff, to work on new projects, and to finish the unfinished works on completed contracts whose site offices have been closed.

**2.4**    The duty of the **planning department** is to plan and coordinate the works so as to make the most economic use of labour, plant and other resources. There are two stages of planning: **tender planning** and **contract planning**. In the tender planning stage, it is necessary to liaise with the estimating department and to provide the latter with a preliminary work programme and method statements (section 2.2). When a tender becomes a contract, it comes to the contract planning stage. It is necessary for the planning department to liaise with the project manager or the site agent and the planning engineer on site (Fig. 2.2) and carry out a detailed contract planning exercise. Detailed work programme and method statements will be established during this stage of the planning exercise. Once the construction work starts, the planning and monitoring of the programme of work will be more in the hands of the site planning engineer.

**2.5**    The **engineering support department** gives technical support to the work sites as well as to the other departments in the head office. It is also involved in the investigation or research work associated with new construction methods or problems of an administrative/managerial nature which are particularly important to the company. Traditionally, the temporary work design, work study and cost control of a project are carried out on site by the site engineer (Fig. 2.2). However, there is a trend towards the centralization of technical functions at the engineering support department in the head office. The reasons for centralization are:
1.    standard designs and procedures can be adopted
2.    a single technical person/team can serve several sites
3.    a head office department can easily access the company's computing facilities for engineering design, cost control and so on, which are usually kept at the head office only

**2.6**    The **plant department** functions as a servicing department in the company, providing plant support to work sites. Its duties are to coordinate all buying, selling and hiring requirements of plant and machinery, to maintain all plant and machinery, and to arrange their transportation to and from construction sites. It is also necessary for the department to liaise with the planning department and the plant engineer on site (Fig. 2.2) giving all information related to plant and machinery during the tender and contract planning stages respectively.

It is normal practice for a contractor to own only those items of plant which are either continuously used or difficult to obtain on hire. However, some very big contracting firms operate their plant department to make profit by letting out plants to other contractors. In such a case, the department usually owns a full range of construction plant. The plant manager (head of this department) will, unlike the former case, report directly to the managing director and works quite independently from the rest of the firm.

**2.7**    The **purchase department** obtains quotations on all materials and subcontractor procurement. At the tendering stage, the purchase department is responsible for liaising with the estimating department so that the necessary cost data are available to the estimator. The department always maintains a full list of the latest costs of materials and subcontracting works and stores it in the firms database. Once a tender is successful, the department will liaise closely with the purchaser on site (Fig. 2.2). Usually, the department invites material suppliers or subcontractors to submit quotations after receiving a requisition from the quantity surveying department (section 2.3). There are four advantages for centralizing purchases at the head office rather than allowing individual site procurement:

1.  a single purchaser can handle purchasing orders for several contracts and so bulk ordering, which is usually cheaper, is possible
2.  the purchaser can obtain substantial discounts by building up long-term relationships and purchasing bulk quantities from suppliers
3.  implementation of a computerized tendering and standardized cost reporting system is possible when all cost information is centralized
4.  administrative support and computing facilities are usually better at the head office

**2.8**   A **contracts manager** is a staff member of the construction division of the company. The department is the most important department in a contracting firm, since the wealth of the company is generated by this department. A contracts manager looks after several projects at any one time. His duties include:

1.  advising the project manager/site agent (Fig. 2.2) on how to organize their work in order to obtain maximum productivity
2.  coordinating and working in conjunction with other servicing departments in the company
3.  attending site meetings
4.  liaising with clients

Because of his importance to the firm, a contracts manager can usually make specific demands on other services departments. He is classified as a member of the head office staff although he spends a lot of time visiting sites under his control. He is a middleman between the senior management of the head office and the site staff. His position demands him to be a man of high calibre. Contracts managers usually become top mangers in a contracting firm.

## 3.   Organization of a Contractor's Site

**3.1**   The organization structures of 12 different contractors' sites in Hong Kong were surveyed. A typical site organization was derived and is shown in Fig. 2.2. This organization chart should be read in conjunction with Fig. 2.1, the typical contractor's head office organization. One should note the relationship between site personnel and head office staff.

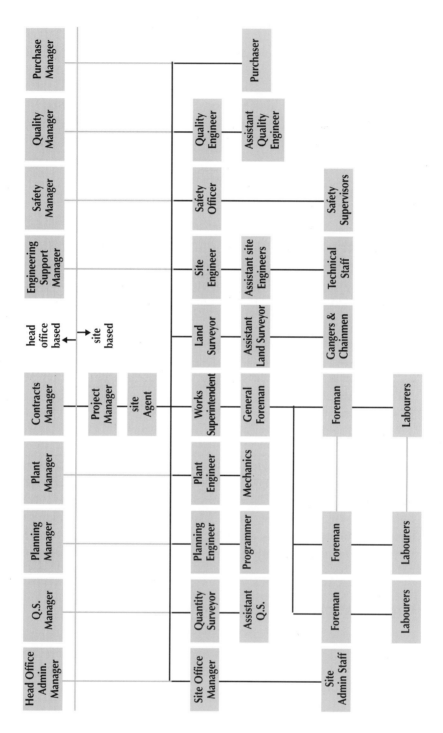

**Fig. 2.2** A typical contractor's organization on a large site.

In Fig. 2.2, it can be observed that project organization exists in a part of the chart, that is, the relationship between the general foreman and the foremen. Besides this, the whole organization is dominantly functional.

3.2    **The project manager/site agent** is the chief person representing the contractor on site. In some relatively small contracts, there is no project manager and the site agent is the top man, whereas in some large contracts, the post of project manager is established and under him is the site agent. The project manager is usually a very experienced person in construction with a very good academic background. The site agent is also a very experienced person but may not have the project manager's very good formal academic background.

Being the chief administrator on site, the project manager/site agent is responsible for directing and controlling all construction work. His main duty is to see that all work is constructed according to the requirements of the contract. As a leader of the construction team he must be able to demonstrate his ability to organize works and to make sound decisions. He should also possess some general sense of how a business is run and how to supervise people.

3.3    The **works superintendent/general foreman** is the key person in controlling the execution of works by mobilizing the labour force as required. Normally, the post of the works superintendent is not established unless the contract is a very huge one. A works superintendent/general foreman is responsible for issuing instructions to the foremen working under him. He advises the site agent about the requirement of materials and the plant engineer about the type of plant needed. He spends most of his time visiting every part of the site everyday.

The works superintendent/general foreman usually has extensive practical knowledge in various construction skills although he is usually not very well academically qualified. He is, however, a key person in transforming a set of construction drawings into finished structures. He should have the ability to read from drawings, to demonstrate to **foremen** and labourers how the work is carried out and to supervise them accordingly. A general foreman is usually promoted from foreman who have been working on site for a long time and have extensive practical construction experience.

**3.4** The **land surveyor** is responsible for the setting out works and for making sure that works are constructed at correct levels. The land surveyor and his gangers and chainmen are the people who actually carry out such works. Sometimes, if the quantity surveyor is too busy, the land surveyor may help him in calculating the volume of excavation/ filling for the earthwork part of the contract. He must be a very careful person and must ensure that no mistake is made in setting out or in levelling works. Such accuracy is most important to the contractor as the latter cannot usually afford the financial consequences due to constructing works at wrong positions or wrong levels.

**3.5** Other key persons in a contractor's site organization are covered in sections 2.3 to 2.7 of this chapter.

## 4. Organization of a Consulting Firm's Head Office

**4.1** Six large consulting firms' head office organization in Hong Kong were surveyed. A typical organization structure was derived and is shown in Fig. 2.3. It is typically a functional organization (section 3 of Chapter 1). Each director has his own specialism. Besides engineering expertise, a director also looks after one or more areas of management, such as human resources or training, for the company.

**4.2** When there is a new project, a design team will be formed. The team leader solicits specialist input from different departments which are headed by the directors. A design team can be as small as two or three persons, or as large as forty or fifty persons, depending on the size of the project.

## 5. Organization of a Consulting Engineer's Representative on Site

**5.1** A consulting firm usually has a representative on site to supervise the contractor who undertakes construction works designed by the former. This representative is called the resident engineer (RE). Nine resident engineers' organization structures in Hong Kong were surveyed. A typical RE's organization was derived and is shown in Fig. 2.4.

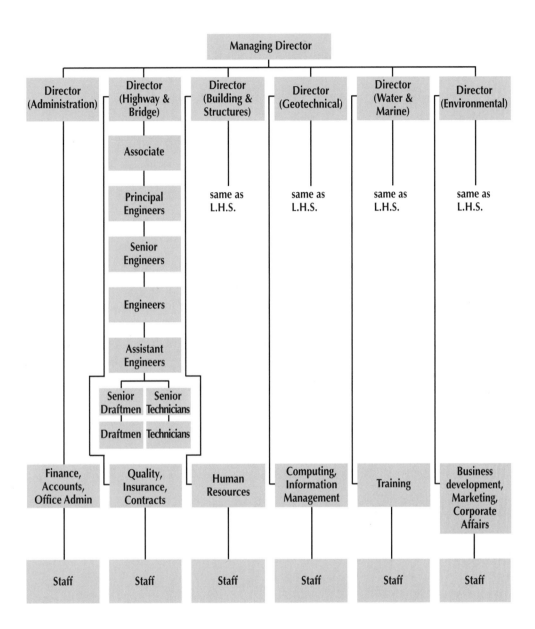

**Fig. 2.3**   A typical large consulting firm's head office organization.

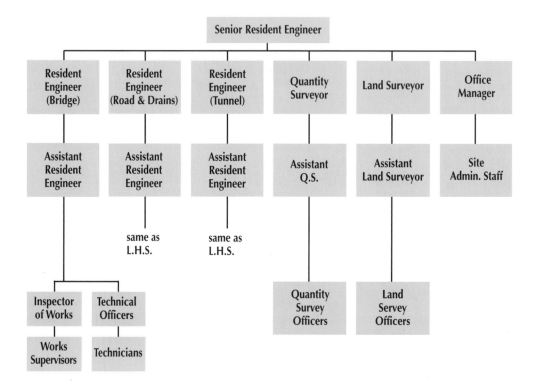

**Fig. 2.4** A typical resident engineer's organization structure.

By comparing Fig. 2.4 with Fig. 1.3 of Chapter 1, one can see that the RE's organization is a matrix organization. It is task-oriented for each of the REs shown in the organization chart but is specialist-oriented for people such as quantity surveyor or land surveyor. The latter give their services to all the REs. Each RE has to look after a specific task.

**5.2** The **resident engineer** is, as mentioned in section 5.1, an agent of the Engineer. He should always be responsible to the Engineer since his decisions may affect the responsibilities and obligations of the latter. Whenever there is any problem or dispute on site between the client and the contractor, the RE must act impartially. Neither the client's nor the contractor's opinion should influence the RE's decision. The basis of the RE's judgement should stem from his professional knowledge.

The main duties of an RE are to supervise the works carried out on site by the contractor and to make sure that the works are constructed according to the contract drawings, that the works completed are of good quality, that the contractor is fairly paid, and that a full set of records about the construction works completed is kept. He is usually a professional person with high academic qualifications, proper professional training and extensive practical experience in supervising construction works.

5.3    The **inspector of works** has the main duties of helping the RE to check the materials and workmanship provided by the contractor and to keep a daily report incorporating all details in connection with the actual progress of works. So, the essential requirement of a competent inspector, besides practical experience and technical knowledge, is the ability to judge quality and workmanship. An inspector of works is technically qualified (for instance, holding a higher certificate) and possesses extensive practical experience in various areas of construction. Sometimes, a contractor's general foreman with the appropriate technical qualification may become an inspector of works if the former wants to work for the RE instead of the contractor.

5.4    The **works supervisor** works under the inspector of works. His duty is to ensure that (by constant checking) the contractor's staff is constructing the works as specified in the contract by using the right amount of suitable materials. He should spend most of his time outside the site office observing and recording progress/production on the spot and ensuring that the contractor's foreman gives proper instructions to the labourers. A works supervisor should have some basic technical training and a few years of site construction experience.

# 3

# CONSTRUCTION CONTRACT I

This chapter will discuss topics such as the meaning of a contract, forms of contract, parties to a contract, and types of contracts. The general meaning of a contract as well as specific characteristics of construction contracts will be dealt with in detail.

## 1. What Is a Contract?

A contract is an agreement between two or more than two parties (individuals or organizations) to perform or not to perform certain acts. This agreement must also be enforceable by law.

A contract can be a 'simple contract' or a 'specialty contract'. Specialty contracts are also commonly referred to as 'contracts under seal'. They will be discussed in more detail in the next section.

## 1.1 Major Requirements of a Contract

- Offer and acceptance
- Consideration
- Form of a contract

### 1.1.1    Offer and Acceptance

The party that makes the offer to do or not to do something is called the 'offeror' and the party to which the offer is made is called the 'offeree'. An offer is an expression of willingness to enter into a contract on certain terms and conditions and can be made orally, in writing, or by conduct. Once the offer is made, the offeree can 'accept' the offer if the terms and conditions are acceptable to that party. Just like an offer, an acceptance may also be made orally, in writing, or by conduct. In the case of construction contracts, the contractor makes the offer through the 'form of tender' and the client (owner, employer) issues the formal acceptance by way of a letter.

### 1.1.2    Consideration

Simple contracts must have 'consideration'. There is no need for consideration to be present in the case of contracts under seal. However, construction contracts that are mostly contracts under seal do have consideration. Thus, for simple contracts it is essential to have consideration while contracts under seal may or may not have consideration.

Consideration may be defined as 'one party providing some goods or services to the other party who in return pays for these goods or services in monetary (financial) terms'. Also, under the 'limitation ordinance', for simple contracts the right to 'sue' (take legal action against another party) is within six years, whereas it is twelve years for contracts under seal. This is the primary reason why most construction contracts are contracts under seal.

A contract under seal is a contract made by a 'deed'. This means that such a contract must be in writing, signed, sealed (official chop), and delivered by the owner (in the case of a construction contract).

### 1.1.3    Form of a Contract

Simple contracts do not need to have any form of contract since they can be made orally, in writing, or by conduct. Because contracts under seal need to be in writing, a form of a contract is necessary. It is always preferable to use one of the standard forms available, rather than to invent one's own personal form. There are, in practice, several private forms that have been established by the large industrial corporations for their own use. In Hong Kong, for example, we have the Hong Kong Standard Form of Contract for use in the private sector. For government projects, standard forms of contracts for building and civil engineering works are issued by the Hong Kong SAR government. The imposition of contracts which are biased in favor of the employer are not recommended. Contractors in such cases will tend to overprice the work, even in times of shortage of work, to cover the additional risks involved. The modification of some of the standard clauses, or the addition of special clauses, should only be made in exceptional cases.

## 2. Parties to a Construction Contract

The main parties to a construction contract are the employer, the consultant (architect, engineer, quantity surveyor, etc.), and the main contractor. A brief description of their roles and responsibilities in the execution of a construction contract is given below.

### 2.1 The Employer

The employer, developer, promoter, owner, or the client — as they may be called in different places — is responsible for the initiation and the financing of new construction projects. Employers may be in the public sector or in the private sector. Public sector owners are basically government agencies/departments and are involved in civil engineering works such as highways, dams, bridges, tunnels, and building works such as schools, libraries, hospitals, etc. Private sector owner is mostly associated with building construction works such as office complexes, hotels, shopping malls, apartment complexes, private housing estates, etc.

Clients in the public sector may be influenced by both social and political trends and needs, and the desire to build may be limited by these factors. The private sector, which encompasses the individual house owner and the large multinational corporation, will probably direct its capital spending to the ventures that are considered to be financially profitable. In recent years there has been emphasis upon obtaining value for money, particularly in the public sector. This has tended to be viewed on a building's life cycle rather than upon initial construction costs alone.

### 2.2 The Architect

The architect has traditionally been the leader of the design team. Because projects today require a large amount of specialized knowledge to complete the design, the architect may require the assistance of consultants from other professional disciplines.

The architect's function is to provide the client with an acceptable and satisfactory building upon completion. This will involve the proper arrangement of space within the building, shape, form, type of construction and materials, environmental controls and aesthetic consideration.

A contractor, who believes that the architect is attempting to exercise powers beyond those assigned under the contract, can insist that the architect specify in writing the conditions that allow such powers. The architect will generally operate under the rules of 'agency' on the part of the employer. This means that instructions given to the contractor will be accepted and paid for by the employer.

In the normal pre-contract stage the architect's duty is to prepare a design for the works. This may involve three facets: architectural design, constructional detailing and contract administration. The architect during the work must exhibit reasonable skill and care in the design of the works. The architect will also generally be held responsible for any work delegated to another.

During the post-contract stage, the work to be undertaken by the architect is largely supervision and administration. Some drawings and details may still need to be prepared, particularly where the contractor requests such information. The purpose of supervision is to ensure that the works are carried out in accordance with the contract documents. The duties of administration are usually to describe the various functions such as issuing instructions to the contractor that must be carried out during the progress of the works.

## 2.3 The Engineer

There is a wide range of different types of engineers employed in a construction project. These may range from civil and structural engineers to building services engineers. Civil engineers are responsible for the design and supervision of civil and public works engineering, and are employed in a similar way to that of architects employed on a building construction project. Their work can be very diverse, and may include projects associated with transportation, energy requirements, sewage schemes or land reclamation projects. The architect on behalf of the client usually employs structural engineers. They act as consultants to design the frame and the other structural members iii buildings. The building services engineers are responsible for designing the mechanical, electrical, HVAC (heating, ventilation, and air-conditioning), and other related systems that are required in today's modern buildings.

## 2.4 The Quantity Surveyor

The quantity surveyor has functions ranging from a measurer to a building accountant and a cost adviser. The emphasis of the quantity surveyor's work has shifted from one solely associated with accounting functions, to one involved in all matters of forecasting financial matters regarding the project.

The initial duty of the quantity surveyor is to forecast and evaluate the design in economic terms both on an initial and life-cycle cost basis. The quantity surveyor must prepare the tendering documentation used by the contractor and, finally report on interim payments and financial progress, and the preparation and control of the final expenditure for the project.

## 2.5 The Main Contractor

A general or main contractor undertakes the majority of the construction work. These firms will vary in size, employing from a few to many thousands of employees. Although there is no clear dividing line between building and civil engineering works, many firms tend to specialize in only one of these sectors.

The smallest building firms may specialize in one trade, and as such may act as either domestic subcontractors or jobbing builders carrying out mainly repairs and small alterations. On the very large projects it is common to find specialist firms for piling, steelwork, tunneling, dredging operations, etc.

The contractors agree to carry out the works in accordance with the contract documents and the instructions from the architect. They agree to do this usually within a stated period of time and for an agreed sum of money. The main contractor must also comply with all statutory laws and regulations during the execution of the work, and ensure that subcontractors, suppliers, and vendors who are employed on the site abide by these conditions too.

## 2.6 The Subcontractor

It is very unusual today for a single contractor to undertake all the construction works with its own workforce. Even in the case of minor building projects, the main contractor is likely to require the assistance of specialist trade firms. Work undertaken by firms other than the main contractor are called subcontractors. When the main contractor has the freedom to choose any subcontractor, then this subcontractor is known as the 'domestic subcontractor' or 'direct subcontractor'. Even in the case of the domestic subcontractor, approval has to be sought from the architect, although it is rare for the approval not to be given. In case the owner (through the architect) specifies certain firms or contractors which the main contractor can employ as subcontractors, then they are called 'nominated subcontractors'.

## 3.    Types of Contracts

When dealing with types of contracts it is important to make a distinction between types of contracts based on 'organizational choices (contractual relationships)' and types of contracts based on 'terms of payment'. As far as organizational choices are concerned, we have a range of contractual arrangements varying from the traditional or conventional contracts at one end of the spectrum to build-operate-transfer (BOT) contracts at the other end.

### 3.1    Contractual Arrangements

The different types of contractual arrangements usually encountered in construction contracts are discussed below.

### 3.1.1   Traditional Contracts

In the traditional contract, the owner has a direct contractual relationship with the main contractor and the consultant. There is no contractual relationship between the consultant and the main contractor or between the owner and the subcontractor. The consultant carries out all the design work in the first instance, prepare the contract documents, and assist the owner in the selection of the main contractor. Thereafter, the construction part of the project gets underway and the supervision of the main contractor's work is usually the responsibility of the consultant (the architect or the engineer, the one who designs the work). The organizational structure of the traditional contractual arrangement is shown in Fig. 3.1.

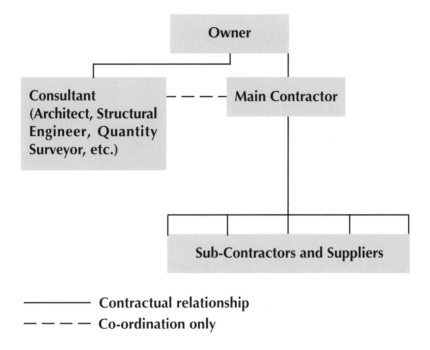

**Fig. 3.1** Traditional contractual arrangement.

Major advantages of using this method is that it is well known to all the participants of the construction project, and provides the best possible price to the client because of open competition. The major disadvantage is that the design of the project has to be completely finished before the tendering and subsequent construction can begin. This method of project delivery takes longer time than other newer contractual arrangements (see below), and is thus not well suited to projects that have to be completed in an emergency manner.

### 3.1.2   Design-Build Contracts

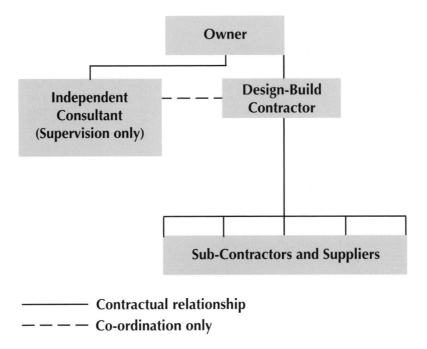

**Fig. 3.2**   Organizational structure of a design-build contract.

In these types of contracts, one firm is given the responsibility of doing both the design and the construction work. The requirements of the project are communicated to the potential design-build contractors through the 'client's brief'. This method is becoming increasingly popular with clients because it offers single point responsibility for clients. The major advantages of using this type of project delivery system are:

1.   better time management
2.   almost negligible adversarial relationship between the designers and the constructors (as both groups belong to the same company)
3.   design-construction overlap, resulting in faster project delivery and hence owners' savings in interest payments for lock-up capital and earlier monetary rewards due to earlier completion

4.  improved constructability and higher functionality of the product as a result of better utilization of the contractor's expertise
5.  better teamwork and price certainty

The major disadvantages include the possible discrepancies between owner requirements and contractor proposals; and fewer choices of contractors, since contractors in design-build contracts must be very experienced so that 'young' contractors may not have the ability to compete. The need for owners (in most cases) to hire independent consultants or supervision teams for the overall supervision of the project may be a disadvantage to some because this incurs extra costs. However, this can also be viewed as an advantage, because under-table deals between the design consultants and the contractors, as may happen in the case of traditional contracting, usually for the sake of hiding consultants' faults (mainly their own design faults), can be avoided. Fig. 3.2 depicts the organizational structure of such a system.

### 3.1.3   Management Contracts

In this arrangement the owner appoints an external organization to coordinate and manage the design and construction phases of a project. The management contractor does not execute any of the construction work itself, rather it tenders out the work in the form of work packages to different subcontractors known as work package contractors. The management contractor receives from the owner a fee for managing all the works. There is a direct contractual relationship between the work package contractors and the management contractor, who in turn has a contractual relationship with the owner. The contracts signed between the management contractor and the work package contractors are usually lump sum or BQ contracts (sections 3.2.1 and 3.2.2), but the contract signed between the owner and the management contractor is usually a cost-plus contract (section 3.2.3).

The management contractor is usually appointed early in the project life and has considerable design input. He tenders out work packages one by one at different times according to the progress of the design work. Once the design of a work package is finished, it can be let out to a work package contractor. Thus the construction work of this particular work package can commence while the design of other work packages is still in progress. Usually the management contractor recognizes the effect of each work package on the overall programme and identifies the sequence of work packages necessary to complete a project. Because of this, savings can be achieved because of design-construction overlap, improved decision-making, which usually are the results of good overall management skills of the management contractor. Cost savings are also possible during the process of selecting work package contractors (or subcontractors), because instead of awarding all works to one single main contractor, the owner can now enjoy the flexibility of having different subcontractors such that cost reduction of each work package becomes easier to achieve. One disadvantage is the requirement of the owner to pay a certain percentage of the contract sum (or sometimes a fixed sum of money) as management fees to the management contractor, and therefore the overall costs will be higher. (This disadvantage, however, can be compensated by the advantages resulted from faster delivery of the project, as discussed in section 3.1.2.) Other disadvantages include the greater risk exposure of the client because of the absence of an overall tender price for the project at the start of work; and a tendency to impose additional administrative burden and some duplication of supervisory staff. The organizational structure is shown in Fig. 3.3.

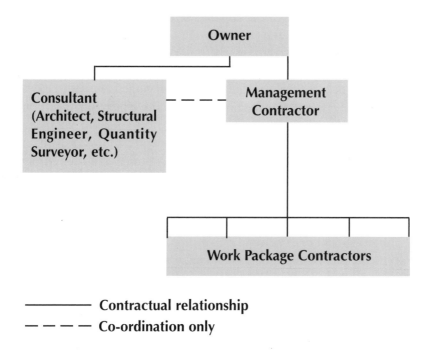

**Fig. 3.3**   Organizational structure of a management contract.

### 3.1.4  Construction Management Contracts

As opposed to the management contracting system that was developed in the United Kingdom, construction management contracting evolved in the United States of America. They are essentially similar to management contract with one noticeable difference. The construction manager (usually a firm) does not have any contractual relationship with the work package contractors, who, on the contrary, have direct contractual relationship with the owner. The construction manager basically acts as the 'agent' of the owner and is responsible for ensuring that the project is completed on time, within budget, and meets the expectations of the stakeholders. Besides this difference, the management contracting and the construction management contracting are basically the same. Fig. 3.4 shows the organizational structure of a construction management contract.

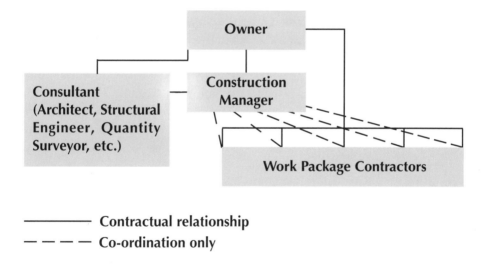

**Fig. 3.4**  Organizational structure of a construction management contract.

### 3.1.5   Build-Operate-Transfer (BOT) Contracts

Also known as build-own-operate-transfer (BOOT), it is one of the fastest ways of privatizing public infrastructure. It is basically a design-build contract but with an extra element - that the contractor (usually a consortium) is also responsible for financing the project. In this method of project delivery, one company is responsible for, as said, arranging all the financing for the project, its design and construction, and finally its operation and maintenance, for a fixed number of years (normally between 20 to 30 years). A BOT contract is a design-build contract in the owner's eyes, plus the additional benefit of utilizing contractor's financing. BOT contracts normally involve projects such as ports, tunnels, power plants, telecommunication networks, highways, dams, etc. They usually require huge amounts of investment and are a good way of developing the infrastructure for cash strapped governments.

Their advantages lie in the fact that clients do not have to worry about financial issues. There is a transfer of equipment and technology, and the project is less risky for the owner. From experiences in Hong Kong, the overlapping in design and construction, and the use of more creative and efficient construction methods for BOT schemes can result in shorter completion time than other types of contracting methods. A better quality of work can also be achieved. Disadvantages primarily are the huge amounts of money that is required to be provided by one company (usually a consortium) and the tremendous political, economic, and environmental risks the consortium has to bear. However, from the owner's (usually the government's) point of view, considerable responsibilities and risks can be passed to the contractors when such schemes are deployed.

BOT projects are important nowadays for two reasons. First, there is a growing trend towards replacing government financing with private sector financing. Second, such projects encourage the principal participants, who are financing the projects besides constructing and managing them, to enhance their overall business success.

## 3.2   Terms of Payment

Based on terms of payment, construction contracts can be classified as being either 'price-based' or 'cost-based'. Price-based contracts include lump sum and unit rate contracts. Cost-based contracts on the other hand include cost-reimbursable and target cost contracts.

### 3.2.1 Lump Sum Contract

This type of contract is based on a single tendered price for the entire works. The contract sum is fixed and agreed before the construction work commences. Where lump sum contracts are to be used, the owners must have a clear idea as to what the project requirements are. Changes and variations during the execution of the project can be extremely costly and time consuming. The contractor is normally paid a portion of the contract sum on completing a major stage of work or milestone.

The major advantage of this type of contract is the high degree of certainty about the final price from the beginning. Also, the evaluation of lump sum tenders is fairly simple and straightforward. Disadvantages include the lack of opportunity for the client to participate in project management and a tendency on the part of the contractor to resort to cost cutting and trivial claims if he feels that he has been burdened with considerable risk.

### 3.2.2 Unit Rate Contract

1. Bill of Quantities Contract

The 'bill of quantities' contract is based upon measuring the actual quantities of work that has been carried out by the contractor and then applying the rates quoted by the contractor in his tender. Payment to the contractor is usually on a monthly basis. A bill of quantities is a list of item of works with a brief description of that work item. Quantities associated with a particular work item are entered in the next column followed by the rate ($/m, $/m^2$, $/m^3$ etc.). Wherever possible, bill of quantities should be prepared using standard descriptions and measurements such as the 'Hong Kong Standard Method of Measurement for Building and Civil Engineering Works'. The use of such contract allows the risks to be shared by the owner and the contractor, and therefore the tender price (contract sum) will tend to be low.

2. Schedule of Rates Contract

A schedule of rates is very similar to bill of quantities with one major difference. For such a contract type, quantities of work are not provided and the contractors are asked to insert rates for the listed items of work. This situation arises in projects where there is a large amount of uncertainty about the expected quantities due to the uncertain scope of work at the time of tendering. The main advantage for this type of contract is that the work can be put to tender before the design is fully completed. However, the down side of this is that the final cost of the project is not known until the project is completed in all respects.

### 3.2.3    Cost-reimbursable (or Cost-plus) Contract

In these types of contracts, the total actual costs of materials, plant, and labor are recorded. To this amount a fee is usually added to cover the contractors management costs, overheads, and profits. Three of the most commonly used contracts of this type are:

1.  cost plus percentage
2.  cost plus fixed fee
3.  cost plus fluctuating (variable) fee

In the cost plus percentage contract, the contractor is reimbursed (paid) the actual cost of material, labour, and equipment (called **prime costs**) along with a predetermined percentage of these costs. In the cost plus fixed fee contract, the prime costs are reimbursed to the contractor plus a fixed fee regardless of the prime costs. In the cost plus fluctuating fee contract, the percentage fee is progressively reduced as the prime costs increase. The greater the prime cost, the lower the percentage for calculating the contractor's fee.

It is worthwhile to note that a management contract — the contract between the owner and the management contractor — is usually a cost-plus contract because the contractor usually receives a fee (either on a percentage basis or on fixed fee basis) from the owner.

The major advantage of using this type of contract is that it can be used in projects which are of an emergency nature, such as remedial works, retrofitting and renovation projects, where the character and scope of the project cannot be easily determined, or where new technology is being used. However, since the client has to bear most of the risks (cost overruns, delays, claims, etc.), there is no incentive for the contractor to perform in an efficient and effective manner. This may be a disadvantage for such a type of contract.

### 3.2.4    Target Cost Contract

These types of contracts are basically a slight variation of the cost-reimbursable contracts. The difference is the fact that both the owner and the contractor agree to an expected (target) cost before the start of the project. This is usually achieved by using a priced bill of quantities for prime costs. Normally any difference (either profit or loss) between the final (actual) cost and the target cost is shared between the owner and the contractor. It must be understood that setting realistic target costs are often not very easy, and care must be taken in this exercise.

# 4

# CONSTRUCTION
# CONTRACT II

In Chapter 3, topics such as the meaning of contracts, requirements of contracts, parties to a construction contract and different types of contracts were discussed. This chapter will provide an introductory discussion on topics like contract documents, tendering procedures, types of contractor's claims and resolution of disputes.

## 1.   Contract Documents

The purpose of the contract documents is to provide sufficient information about the project to the prospective tenderers. Contract documents should be concise and precise, and present a clear picture of the division of responsibilities and legal obligations between the parties. This will enable them (the contractors) to properly assess the risks involved and submit realistic offers. The contract documents under any construction project should at least include the following information.

## 1.1   Instructions to Tenders

These are usually the first part of the contract documents. They include information on the unique features of the work and the procedure to be followed in submitting bids (tenders). This ensures that all bids are properly prepared and delivered, and that they can be evaluated on the same criteria.

## 1.2   Form of Tender

It is the formal offer of the contractor to execute the contract in accordance with the various contract documents for a specified contract sum. Once this form is completed and submitted, the tenderer is assumed to have acknowledged the presence and acceptance of other contract documents such as the drawings, specifications, bill of quantities, etc.

## 1.3   Conditions of Contract

They define generally the constraints under which the work is to be undertaken, the contractual relationship between the client and the contractor, the rights and responsibilities of the client and the contractor, the powers of the Engineer and their limitations, etc. Also known as general conditions, they contain detailed clauses regarding payment to the contractor, mechanism for the application and the subsequent approval for extension of time (EOT), liquidated damages, defects liability, damage to public property, etc. They also include a definition of the 'terms' used in the contract so that there is no ambiguity about the identity of the parties.

## 1.4   Drawings

They are the graphic presentation of the extent and details of the works that are to be actually constructed on site. They are used to communicate the designer's ideas about the construction methods and sequence to the contractors. They are also used for record purposes and can be a valuable tool in resolving disputes between the different parties in case of confusion.

The contract drawings should ideally be completed and finalized at tender stage. This is, however, not always the case. Usually there is insufficient time for the pre-contract design work, or indecision on the part of the client and the design team. The contract drawings will normally include the general arrangement drawings showing the site location, the position of the building on the site, means of access to the site, floor plans, elevation and sections.

## 1.5   Specifications

They are used to describe the nature, quality, and class of materials and workmanship required and state any constraints as to the methods of construction so as to control the quality of all end products in the work. Secondly they can also he used to cover any specific conditions of contract that are not a part of the general conditions. The most common types of specifications used in the construction industry are the design specifications, technical specifications, product specifications and the performance specifications.

## 1.6    Bill of Quantities

They are prepared from the drawings/specifications and fully describe the work that has to be earned out. It is in the form of a systematic and recognized list of items of work and represents the breakdown of all materials, labours and plans required for the completion of the project. A bill of quantities allows each contractor tendering for a project to price the work using the same information.

The bill may include firm or approximate quantities depending on the completeness of drawings and other information from which it was prepared. Although the main purpose of the bill of quantities is to assist the contractor in the preparation of his tender, it can be used for many other purposes such as preparation of interim valuations, valuations of variations and preparation of final accounts, etc.

## 1.7    Work Programme (Schedule)

It is submitted by the contractor, usually in the form of a bar chart (usually supported by CPM network diagrams). It describes the relationship of interdependent activities and duration of each activity involved in the work, together with the overall contract time. Schedules generally improve communication between the architect and the builder. They are also of immense help to the quantity surveyor in preparing the bills of quantities. They can also be utilized in the placement of orders for materials and equipment. Lastly, it is a very important document for supporting contractual claims or disputes (Chapter 16).

## 1.8    Articles of Agreement

This is the formal contract signed by the parties, which hinds all the contract documents together. It should be noted that the contract is between the employer and the contractor. The blank spaces in the articles of agreement are filled with the names of the employer, the architect/engineer, and the main contractor; the name of the works; date of signing the contract: and the names and signatures of the witnesses. If the parties make any changes to these Articles of Agreement or to any other part of the contract, then both parties should acknowledge this alteration.

## 2.    Tendering Procedures

When the design team has almost or fully completed the design of the works, the next step in the process is the selection of the contractor(s) to carry out the construction work. The three most common methods of selecting a contractor are the open tendering, selective tendering and the negotiated tendering procedures.

### 2.1    Open Tendering

In this procedure, practically any contractor can submit a bid for the job. The general procedure is that the client or the client's consultants will place an advertisement in the gazette (in the case of public projects), trade magazines and newspapers highlighting the significant features of the project, such as the nature and scope of the works, rough estimate of cost of the works, the time available, and the location of the site.

This method of tendering has the benefit of attracting the largest number of tenders and hence the prices obtained are usually very competitive. The procedure gives the impression of being fair, since it allows virtually any contractor to bid for the job. On the negative side, every tender must be scrutinized, not only to ensure that its contents are satisfactory but also to ensure that the tenderer is technically and financially sound and capable. Also, when a large number of contractors are asked to submit their tenders, a lot of time and effort is put into unsuccessful tenders and it proves to be a burden for the industry.

### 2.2    Selective Tendering

The disadvantages of open tendering can be overcome by the use of selective tendering. Selective or limited tendering may be exercised in one of two ways: either by advertising for firms to indicate their interest and then short-listing them, or by selecting from a standing list of approved firms. In the former, the contractors are asked to submit documents to show the types and scope of work they have undertaken in the past, and their technical, financial and managerial capabilities. This process is known as 'prequalification'. In the second case, the list is usually prepared from the experience of the clients and the consultants regarding the different contractors who are active in that area of work. In the selective tendering procedure, normally five to seven contractors are invited to submit their tenders for the intended project.

## 2.3    Negotiated Tendering

The purpose of this method of selecting a contractor to decide on an acceptable tender after detailed discussions and meetings between the client and the contractor. There are two ways in which this can be accomplished. First, in cases where the scope of the work is uncertain, the project has to start at the earliest possible date, or a client may have preference for certain contractors, then the client will invite a few contractors to submit their proposals and then a contractor will be selected after a few rounds of discussions and negotiations. These negotiations will mainly focus on the time, cost, and quality aspects of the work. Second, there may be an initial round of competitive tendering and then two or three contractors may be invited by the clients for further negotiations on certain key aspects of the project. Final selection will then be made after both parties agree to a mutually beneficial arrangement.

## 3.    Contractual Claims

Claims from contractors generally arise when they feel that they are eligible for additional payments by the owner because of the occurrence of certain factors. The most common claims submitted by the contractor during the process of the contract are claims for fluctuations, delays, extension of time, and direct loss and/or expense.

## 3.1    Fluctuations

Fluctuations refer to the changes in the price of materials and wages during the course of a construction project. In most cases, the prices of materials and wages increase because of inflationary effects. Most forms of contracts will provide for some sort of mechanism to deal with this issue. In Hong Kong, the Hong Kong Standard Form allows for increases or decreases in wage rates only by the provision of a relevant clause.

The Census and Statistics Department of the Hong Kong government publishes the Index of Rates including labour wages and material costs for the Building Industry every month. The fluctuations in the rates are based on this publication.

## 3.2 Delays

This is one of the most contentious issues in the construction industry. It is by far the most common cause of dispute between the two parties and almost always result in claims. Claims for delays can be further split into three sections depending on the party responsible for causing the delay.

### 3.2.1 Delays Caused by the Main Contractor

The delays caused by the main contractor are usually due to poor management skills of the contractor. Such delays are generally due to improper coordination of subcontractors and suppliers/vendors, late delivery of materials, labour shortages, and insufficient or unsuitable plant, etc.

### 3.2.2 Delays Caused by the Owner

In a large number of cases, this category of delays has been quite predominant. Owners generally make a lot of changes during the execution of the construction projects, which invariably result in the project time estimate to be revised upwards. These delays are also due to the failure of the architect in supplying the construction drawings, site instructions, and other details.

### 3.2.3 Delays Caused by Neither Party

Circumstances sometimes arise which cause delays in the project but they cannot be attributed to any single party. In other words neither party has any control of the situation. These are referred to as 'force majeure'. They include events such as the outbreak of war, epidemics, and major natural catastrophes such as earthquakes, cyclones, etc.

## 3.3 Extension of Time

When failure to complete the project according to the original schedule is caused by a delay which is outside the control of either party or a delay which is due to the architect's or owner's fault, then the main contractor may apply for an extension of time. Force majeure, unusually bad weather conditions, labour strikes and general unrest, delay due to the nominated subcontractor or nominated supplier, and unforeseeable labour and materials shortages are classified as delays which are the fault of neither party. Delays due to extra/additional work, late issuance of drawings and specifications, and unreasonable and uncalled for inspection of works are caused by the owner.

## 3.4 Claims for Direct Loss and/or Expense

When the contractor cannot earn a profit due to the unnecessary disruption of works caused by the owner or the owner's representatives, or due to variations, then this is termed as a 'loss' to the contractor. In cases where the main contractor has to increase expenditure on some items of work due to disruption and variation to achieve similar results, they are known as 'expense'. The claims under this heading usually include material cost, costs associated with disruption and disturbance of labour, inflation, and main (head) office overheads.

## 4. Resolution of Disputes

One of the key factors in avoiding claims and disputes is to ensure completion of the design in all respects before the start of construction. By this the owner knows exactly what to expect of the end product and can also check to see if the owner's requirements are met. In case the owner is uncertain about his needs, the architect can incorporate a certain degree of flexibility in the design to cater for possible options. Another factor that can reduce claims and disputes is adequate and properly conducted site investigations. If unforeseen ground conditions are revealed at a late stage, they can be disastrous to the overall project aims and objectives.

Moreover, experienced site personnel should always supervise the construction process. Very often, inefficient supervision of the contractor's progress has resulted in the generation of claims. Proper and timely instructions, scrutiny of the quality of workmanship and appropriate records are important ingredients in avoiding claims.

The designer should estimate the cost of construction when the designs are complete and tenders are received. An experienced engineer should be able to do it with a fair degree of accuracy. Any tender that appears to be unusually low in price should be checked for error, as the bidder might have misunderstood the contract. However, the contractor selection process should lay emphasis on competence rather than price alone. No type of contract and no level of supervision can force an incompetent contractor to fully satisfy the owner, as far as meeting the project objectives of time, cost and quality are concerned.

## 4.1    Litigation

This is a process where the disputes between the parties are resolved though the 'courts'. This method is by far the most unpopular way of resolving a dispute in the construction industry, since it almost always involves large amounts of time and money. The party that initiates the legal proceeding against the other party is called 'plaintiff' and the party against whom the legal action is taken is called the 'defendant'. Litigation is now increasingly being replaced by other methods such as arbitration and alternative dispute resolution (ADR).

## 4.2    Arbitration

Arbitration is an alternative to litigation that is quite popular in the construction industry. An arbitration clause is included in the Hong Kong Standard Form of contract and provides a forum for dispute resolution that is less expensive and time consuming than litigation. In this process, an 'arbitrator', chosen by the parties themselves, settles a formal dispute. No lawyers or courts are involved. The arbitrator can be one or two persons. If the arbitrator fails to concur to a decision, a third person called an 'umpire' is appointed to break the deadlock. The decision made by the arbitrator is known as the 'award'. Once the parties involved agreed to this method of settling a dispute, they cannot then take legal action.

## 4.3    Alternative Dispute Resolution

This method has been developed in the last twenty years or so and is considered the best possible alternative way of resolving disputes and disagreements in the construction industry. An ADR is a voluntary process in which the parties are assisted in solving their disputes by a neutral third party without the need of a judge or arbitrator. ADR techniques are (a) mediation, (b) conciliation, (c) adjudication, and (d) executive tribunal. ADR procedures, unlike litigation and arbitration, are not binding until a mutually agreed settlement is reached and is put in writing. That is to say that either party can resort to other methods of dispute resolution if the ADR procedure fails.

### 4.3.1 Mediation

Mediation is a voluntary process (which either side may abandon at any time without prejudice), whereby each side to a dispute is brought together before a neutral 'mediator', whose function is to assist the parties to arrive at a common position by joint open session and private meeting. The mediator plays an active role by putting forward suggestions and encouraging discussions on key issues. When an agreement is reached, it is put in writing for the parties to sign.

### 4.3.2 Conciliation

Conciliation is procedurally similar to mediation. However, the 'conciliator' plays more of a passive role once he has explained the points of views of the one party to another. The conciliator's role is more of a 'facilitator' than a decision-maker.

### 4.3.3 Adjudication

This method differs slightly from the other two in that the outcome of the proceedings is somewhat binding on the parties. The adjudicator's decision can be considered to be a final binding decision if the parties agree or can be used as a basis for further negotiations.

### 4.3.4 Executive Tribunal (Mini Trial)

This method is a more formal undertaking and involves a neutral adviser along with representatives of the parties involved in the dispute. The independent and impartial advisor takes control of the proceedings and acts as an advisor to the parties in dispute. Witnesses are also sometimes called upon to give evidence. Once an agreement is reached it is put in writing for endorsement by the parties concerned.

### 4.3.5 Advantages and Disadvantages of ADR

The strengths of ADR are cost savings, better control of the whole process, mutually agreed decision, continuity of business relationships and confidentiality as the whole process is carried out in private. The 'awards' are also not open to the public. The disadvantages are the non-binding nature of the settlement (until an agreement is signed) and the notion that the suggestion to resolve a dispute through ADR may be viewed as a sign of weakness by the other party.

# 5

# ESTIMATING AND TENDERING

## 1.  Introduction

It is vital for a contracting firm to secure sufficient construction contracts through tendering. Depending on the nature of work, availability of time, client's requirement and type of contractual arrangement, different approaches in estimating and tendering are required. For a lump sum contract based on specifications and drawings, contractors may have to prepare their own bills of quantities in the first place. Tendering based on the government published schedule of rates, however, requires an overall percentage adjustment to the rates for different trades. As selective competitive tendering is the most common way to award a contract, estimating the cost with a high degree of accuracy is of the utmost importance in ensuring that the firm will win the contract with a sufficient margin.

Estimating is defined as the technical process of predicting the cost of construction. Tendering is a separate and commercial function based upon the net cost estimate, adding appropriate mark-up to cover profit and risk to make the lowest offer to carry out the defined work under prescribed conditions for a stated sum of money.

Estimation is more than the simple calculation of cost. An estimate is a prediction of the most likely outcome with judgement of probabilities and risk. Before an estimate is performed, adequate data should have been provided to form a basis for the calculation. Estimation is also a management function because the process of producing an estimate for a tender is a complex one which involves many personnel within and outside the construction company. In a building contract, estimating and tendering are predominantly carried out by a quantity surveyor. However, the input of experienced engineers would be required in civil engineering contracts.

The tender price is based on the cost estimate. The final figure in the tender can reflect the profit or deficit for a particular contract. If the estimate is not accurate enough, it can result in major problems for the contractor who is awarded the contract. The basic components of an estimate for a tender are:

## 1.    Direct Cost

Direct costs are predominantly the labour, material, plant and subcontractor cost involved in executing the works. The direct cost includes allowance for material wastage, handling charge, plant idle time, temporary works, falsework and consumable materials not built into the permanent works.

## 2.    Indirect Cost

Indirect costs are costs which can be directly attributable to a contract and include site staff salary, transport costs, site office cost, insurance and bonds.

It is not always easy to distinguish between direct and indirect costs for items such as the plant cost. The cost of a backhoe can form part of the excavation costs (direct cost) whereas the tower crane used for material delivery can be considered as an item of the core plant and be included in the preliminaries.

## 3.    Mark-up/Profit

The direct cost plus the indirect cost form the 'cost estimate'. The total sum presented in a tender is the contractor's 'selling price'. The difference between the selling price and the cost estimate is the mark-up which usually covers three elements: the company's overhead, the risk and the profit.

This chapter outlines the typical activities in estimating and tendering by a contractor. Fig. 5.1 shows the key activities.

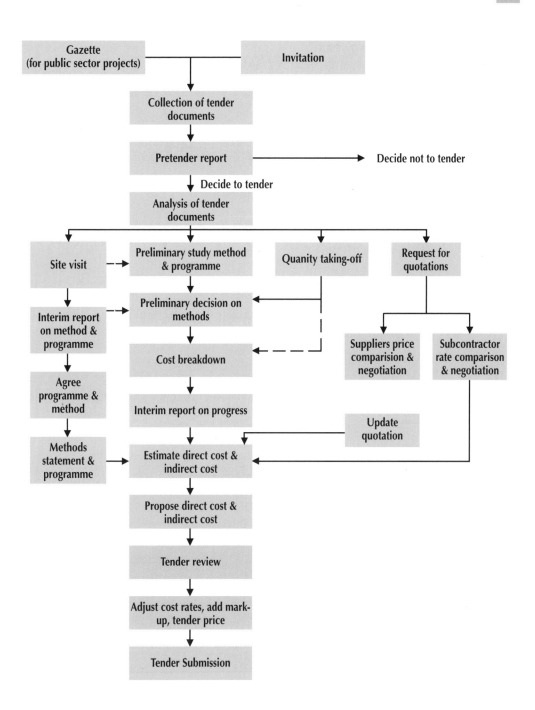

**Fig. 5.1**   Key activities in estimating for tendering.

## 2    Estimating Process

### 2.1    Tender Preparation Authorized by the Senior Management

Upon receipt of an invitation to tender, the estimator is required to register the tender in the 'Register of Tenders' which records the following:

1.    Project location
2.    Title of the project
3.    Employer or client
4.    Estimated cost
5.    Tender closing date
6.    Name of the estimator

Further information, as listed in the 'Authority to Tender' form (Fig. 5.2) is to be compiled by the estimator after reading the tender documents and relevant correspondence. The completed form is checked for accuracy, signed by the estimator and distributed to the senior management.

A tender selection meeting will be held to review the current and prospective tenders and subsequently to decide upon which tenders are to be given approval to proceed, in particular when there are several invitations to tender.

**Information generally included in the 'Authority to Tender' form:**

1. Description/location
2. Client
3. Designer
4. Work Value
5. Profit Level
6. Type of Tender
7. Type of Conditions of Contract
8. Contract Period
9. Maintenance Period
10. Liquidated Damages
11. Escalation Period
12. Payment Terms
    - Method
    - Frequency
    - Period for Issue of Certificate
    - Period for Payment
    - Retention Amount
13. Security Performance Amount
    - Bank Guarantee
    - Insurance Bond
14. Insurance
    - Whole of Works
    - Works Compensation
    - Insurance Bond
15. Estimator
16. Bid Date/Time
17. Bid Deposit/Place
18. Bid Validity Period
19. Review Date
20. Competitor

**Fig. 5.2** Information included in 'Authority to Tender' form.

## 2.2    Programming for Estimating

Following receipt of the tender documents and drawings, the estimator will check to ensure all the items in the 'Tender Checklist' have been included in the client's register.

The estimator will prepare a programme of the tasks required to complete the estimate and establish a list of key dates against which progress can be monitored. This is to ensure that all works are given adequate attention within the limited time available as the deadline for tender submission is precisely defined.

## 2.3    Preliminary Project Study

The estimator will carry out a study of the tender documents and gain an appreciation of the following:

1. Who is the client?  Private sector or the Hong Kong SAR government departments?  Their previous attitude towards supervision of works.
2. Scope of the work and the contractor's experience.
3. The contractual arrangement and risks.
4. Possible construction methods and special resource requirements.
5. Adequacy of the documents. Are the bills of quantities available and what are the principal quantities of work?
6. Tender team requirements. Any specialist/proprietary works and any requirements for contractor's design?
7. Site visit requirements.

The potential for developing and submitting an alternative design should be discussed during the initial tender review meeting. It is useful for the contractor to review any particular area which requires specialist work such as foundation design and availability of resources including experienced personnel, special plant etc. to meet with the technical and commercial requirements. Other considerations are:

1. Method statement and associated temporary works
2. Quality and safety management system
3.  Project schedule

## 2.4 Material and Subcontractor Enquiries

Due to the limited time available at the tendering stage, it is a good practice to issue material and subcontractor enquiries as early as possible. To enable this to be done it is essential for the estimator to follow these steps:

1. To add all bill items containing similar types of work in order to establish the principal quantities of work in each trade.
2. Roughly estimate the cost of the whole project by using the all-in rate for the major items of work.
3. To establish the key delivery dates for materials and subcontractors.
4. To abstract and list all specifications, drawings and bill items relevant to the trade of work, and to prepare enquiries.

### 2.4.1 Material Enquiries

The estimator is usually required to obtain a quoted price for every major material on each tender because of the effect of inflation, variance in delivery cost, and the discount on quantity ordered. Also the estimator needs to consider the availability of required materials, e.g. sources of aggregates, especially during a boom time in the construction industry and the time for delivery of materials or components manufactured abroad. The prices between suppliers, such as the cost of ready-mixed and site-mixed concrete, are compared.

Quotations from suppliers and subcontractors are required for the following reasons:

1. The estimator can obtain the latest prices for materials and labours that reflect the current market conditions.
2. The quotations can be used to check against the estimate prepared by the tendering team and to spot any significant variances.
3. The subcontractors, because of their experience and previous involvement, usually have a better appreciation of the construction problem involved in a particular trade and are more capable to reflect the real cost in the quotations submitted.
4. The subcontractor can suggest realistic solutions to particular problems for the work concerned.
5. Negotiation with subcontractors can result in keen competition in price and ensure that the main contractor will have the costs covered.

It is common for the estimator to assume a price for the required material and proceed with his cost calculation before receiving the quotation. The assumed price is based on recent quotations for other projects and the estimator's knowledge of current market price. When the actual quotation is received, the estimator's calculation will be adjusted to take into account the difference between the assumed price and the actual quotation.

Large construction firms keep updated cost data that the estimator can use to prepare cost estimates irrespective of the subcontractor's quotation. This eliminates the company's dependence on subcontractors in the estimating process.

Enquiries sent to suppliers include:

1.  The location of the project
2.  The specification of the material used for construction
3.  Quantity of the material
4.  The delivery programme and the daily requirement
5.  Method of transport  by land or by sea
6.  Deadline of quotation required
7.  Closing date of the tender
8.  Name of the person of the contracting firm to whom any reference concerning the enquiry should be addressed

After receiving the quotations, the estimator will check whether the material meets the specification as stated in the contract documents and can be delivered to the site at the times required by the construction programme, and also the contractual conditions of supply is satisfactory in terms of payment and validity period of the supplier's offer.

### 2.4.2   Subcontractors' Enquiries

The subcontractor quotations will take more time to prepare. Prior to preparing the request for subcontractor's quotation, the estimator may discuss with the planning department to ascertain the most efficient and practical way of splitting the construction work. This is more relevant for civil engineering projects which are of a one-off nature. Quotations must be compared and negotiated with subcontractors to obtain the best prices which are vital to the success of a tender. Generally, the rates for the selected subcontractors will include both the allowance for attendance and other services. It is seldom for the estimator to assume a price for subcontractor's rates; usually the estimator waits until the actual quotations arrive before including them in the estimate.

In Hong Kong, the main contractors usually sublet most of the works and mainly perform the function of coordination. Factors that dominate the decision of subcontracting are:

1. The specialization of the work involved and size of the contract
2. The financial risk in undertaking the work
3. The work load of the company in order to optimize the resources available
4. Subletting may be required by the client, i.e. nominated subcontracting

Matters that should be explicitly described in the subcontractor's enquiry are:

1. Location and programme of subcontract work
2. Clear definition of scope of works for a particular subcontract
   (This is extremely important for the future administration of the contract, for both the main contractor and the subcontractor. Unclear demarcation between subcontracts leads to additional costs incurred by the main contractor, e.g. Who is responsible for the preparation of concrete surface prior to painting? The concreting subcontractor or the painter?)
3. The subcontractor's responsibilities with respect to making good other work
4. Facilities provided by the main contractor should be stated, such as during delivery of materials within the construction site, use of water and electricity, insurance, material storage areas, access (subcontractor may have to use areas possessed by another subcontractor), scaffolding, etc.
5. Any fluctuation clause for the subcontract?
6. Any warranty/guarantee and control information to be provided by the subcontractor?
7. Any design requirement regarding the specialist works?
8. Safety and other related regulations must be observed on site

The relevant sections of conditions of contract and specification are forwarded to the subcontractor with a copy of the drawings. To avoid the delay in receiving the quotations, early issue of enquiries is essential. Sometimes, it may be costly to send every subcontractor a set of drawings. In such a case, a set of drawings should be available in the main contractor's office for the subcontractor's inspection.

The estimator must check carefully the quotation received on all items that have been priced and correctly extended, and totalled in accordance with the unit of measurement required. The offer with the cheapest price does not imply it will be automatically accepted. Negotiation with subcontractors may result in lower prices. It is wise to know the extent of work the subcontractors have included in their price. Abnormal rates in the quotation should be spotted and the subcontractors should be asked for the reasons of these abnormalities. Subcontractor's quotations may contain qualifications and even unpriced portion of works which they are not interested in or which they do not have enough resources to undertake.

When a subcontractor's quote has been selected, the estimator should check whether an appropriate attendance and site overhead costs should be added to the subcontractor's price with respect to the relevant contract specifications.

Attendance cost consists of the following:

1.  Temporary works such as steel scaffolding
2.  Accommodation facilities, sanitary and welfare facilities
3.  Storage space for plant and materials
4.  Lighting, power, water and other services
5.  Loading and unloading arrangement for materials
6.  Clearing of rubbish

The estimator must have a thorough understanding of the contract programme and the subcontracting requirements during the course of building up the estimates.

### 2.4.3   Differences Between Supplier's and Subcontractor's Quotation

Material prices are usually combined with plant and labour cost to produce the rate in the bill of quantities, whereas the subcontractor's rates may stand on their own together with an allowance for attendance. However, quotations from subcontractors may also require further adjustment. Labour-only subcontracting requires the inclusion of material costs. Quotations having an all-in-rate may also require further adjustment for items outside the responsibility of the subcontractors. Discount or rate adjustment may be obtained after negotiation with the subcontractors.

Generally material prices will be received before the subcontractor's price. The price of items build up is always delayed by the subcontractors' quote. However, some suppliers' quotations could come late, especially for materials manufactured abroad.

## 2.5    Project Study, Method Statement and Planning

Project study is a process of continual refinement and revisions through the whole estimating and tendering period until the tender is submitted. The estimator and the planning engineer should work together to choose the most efficient and the cheapest construction method. They must gain a full appreciation of the work involved in the project by:

1. Studying the tender drawings
2. Integrating the analysis of the bill of quantities and other contract documents
3. Conducting a site visit
4. Raising queries with the client
5. Preparing a method statement and a programme

### 2.5.1   Study and Analysis of Contract Documents

Factors to be considered in the study and analysis of contract documents are:

1. Any special requirements in the Specification, especially the particular specification?
2. Any major discrepancies between the documents? Any works shown on the drawing but not measured in the bills of quantities?
3. Any information not shown in the tender documents?
4. Any particular constraint applicable to the site, such as noise level control, height control etc.?
5. Any site investigation report available for inspection?

An initial analysis of the bill should be performed to produce the principal quantities of each trade or class of work so that an approximate cost can be established at an early stage. The initial analysis may need to be refined after the site visit.

### 2.5.2   Site Visit

Site visit is essential for the estimator and the planning engineer to have a clear understanding of the actual conditions to which suitable measure and adjustment can be included. The estimator has to take photographs of the site and the accesses for discussion during the tender meeting with the senior management. In addition, a 'site visit report' is required to be completed by the estimator after the visit. Fig. 5.3 shows the contents of a typical site visit report.

## SITE VISIT REPORT

**TENDER:**

**SITE LOCATION:**

**1. EXISTING SITE DETAILS:**
- Buildings
- Utility Services
- Obstructions/ restraints to site operations
- Fencing, hoarding
- Trees, streams, graves
- Accessibility: road, sea and public transport
- Traffic conditions on access roads
- Parking restrictions/nearest available

**2. EXISTING BUILDINGS:**
- Temporary support, demolition
- Type of adjacent buildings:  residential, industrial, commercial, others

**3. GROUND CONDITIONS:**
- Topography
- Geotechnical  conditions, borehole locations, type of surface soil, stability, visible water table
- Soil Storage: location, drainage, disposal

**4. AVAILABLE SERVICES:**
- Telephone, gas, water, electricity & gas
- Drains

**5. OTHER SERVICES:**
- Suppliers: ready mixed concrete, quarries
- Refuse tips: distance, charges, exclusions

**6. OFFICE/STORAGE:**
- Offices/Storage:  position, services, movement
- Access roads/Hardstanding

**7. POLLUTION RISKS:**
- Water, noise, air

**Fig. 5.3**  Contents of a site visit report.

Points to be noted during the visit are:

1. Location of site, urban or rural?
2. Topography of the site
3. Any underground services
4. Access problem
5. Nature of ground /soil, possibility of presence of rock and existing foundations?
6. Water table?
7. Adjoining buildings?

### 2.5.3    Raising Queries With the Client

During the assessment of the tender documents, queries may arise relating to the tender documents. The estimator will prepare a list of queries to be forwarded to the client or the engineer.

Upon receipt of the replies to questions raised, the estimator should circulate the copies to ensure the client's requirements are clearly understood by all members of the tender team.

In many cases a pretender meeting will be organized and chaired by the architect or the engineer. All tendering parties will be invited to attend. The architect or the engineer will brief the project and answer queries raised by the tenderers. Tender addendum will be issued to all tendering parties to incorporate any clarifications and changes.

### 2.5.4    Preparing Method Statement and Programme

Method statements are descriptions of how the construction work will be executed, with details of labour and plant required. The estimator and the planning team are responsible for preparing the programme and the method statement. During the course of preparing these documents, they need to consult the site staff, plant managers and temporary works designers.

A pre-tender programme is subject to continual refinement and modification when the estimator and planning team become more and more aware of the implications of the project details. The amount of detailed information incorporated in the tender programme depends on the time available and the keenness of the contractor to win the contract.

Fig. 5.4 illustrates the preparation work for estimating.

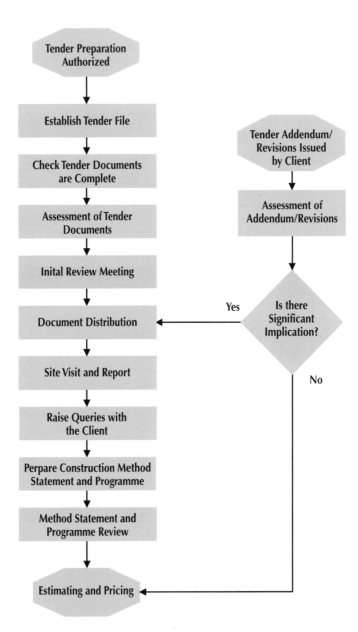

**Fig. 5.4** Preparation work for estimating.

## 2.6    Calculation of 'All-in' Labour Rate and Plant Rate

The hourly cost of 'all-in' labour rate, the plant rate and all numerous expenses resulting from employment of labour need to be established. The main elements to be determined include the following:

1.  The site working hours
2.  The actual hours worked in the year
3.  The non-productive time
4.  The cost of employing labour
5.  The annual cost of labour
6.  Allowances for MPF, annual leave, travelling, tea, etc.

In general, these elements will be affected directly by the contract period, the site location and the current labour market. The rates calculated vary with different contracts and require adjustment by the estimator.

The 'all-in' plant rate depends on the method of acquisition. Plant can be either supplied by the contractor's own plant department or hired from external plant companies. The quoted price from a plant company must be checked, whether or not it has already included the running cost of the machine, the cost of the operator, fuel oil and grease, and other consumables.

For a bought plant, the hourly rate is based on the elements below:

1.  The initial cost
2.  The resale value
3.  Average working hours per year
4.  Life of the machine
5.  Insurance premium per year
6.  Licence and tax per year
7.  Fuel oil and grease cost
8.  Maintenance and repair cost
9.  Required rate of return on the capital

Usually the plant department will produce the calculation and suggest to the estimator but adjustment must be performed to cater for special circumstances in each contract.

## 2.7    Estimation of Direct Cost

The determination of direct cost rate for each item in the bill of quantities involves the selection of appropriate resource of labour, plant and materials. The output and the usage rate for both the labour and plant, the wastage for material together with the unit cost of resources will produce a direct cost for the work.

The output rate and usage rate are based on:

1. Experienced judgement
2. Necessary assumption
3. Logical sequence in the programme
4. Particular site condition

## 2.8    Estimation of Indirect Cost

The indirect cost of an item of work includes the following:

1. Supervision and site management
2. Plant and equipment for material transportation
3. Site services such as water, telephone, electricity and fuel
4. Small tools, survey equipment
5. Testing and commission
6. Site expenses, stationery, computer, furniture and so on
7. Miscellaneous such as employment of the Independent Checking Engineer
8. Buildings for contractor (site office, canteen, workshop)
9. Plant mobilization and utilities
10. Clearance of site
11. Insurance and fees for bonds, etc.

The total of the estimated indirect cost indicates the level of overhead support required for the project. The rate for each of the elements above must be checked and care must be taken to avoid the missing of any item.

As the definition of indirect cost may be different for different companies, some of the items above may be included as direct cost for other firms. The essence of estimation is to ensure that the cost will sufficiently cover all items for the execution of work.

After calculating the indirect cost, the estimator is required to submit a report and present it to the senior management. The contents of the report include:

1. Brief description of the project
2. Method of construction
3. Any unresolved or contractual problem
4. Major assumptions made in the preparation of estimate
5. Any unusual risks in the project

6. Break down for items make up
7. Resource break down and plant, labour, material and subcontractor total
8. Provisional sum and contingencies

Fig. 5.5 is a flowchart depicting the estimating procedures.

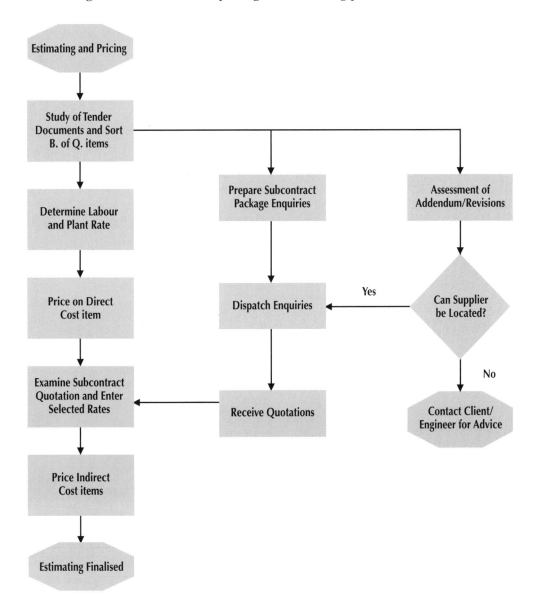

**Fig. 5.5** Estimating procedures.

## 3 Tendering Process

The tendering process is a commercial function based on the net cost estimate with appropriate profit and risk added to make an offer.

### 3.1 Assessment and Adjustment of Estimate

Upon receiving of the report prepared by the estimator, the senior management assesses the estimate and decides the adjustments to be made. The assessment is done by analysing the report and integrating the assumptions made by the estimator. Usually the adjustment is made as a lump sum addition or subtraction.

### 3.2 Allowance for Overheads, Risk and Profit

Construction of a project must contribute towards the cost of running the company's head office and other general overheads of the organisation. The overhead to be included in each tender is based on the latest monthly monitoring of the company's turnover and expenditure.

The risk included in a tender depends on the assessment of:

1. Who is the client?
2. The preliminary items in the bill
3. Work to be undertaken directly by the contractor and work to be subcontracted
4. Contractor's experience with the type of project he is tendering
5. The nominated supplier and subcontractor
6. Fluctuation in labour availability
7. Forecast of likely rise or fall in material and labour costs
8. Lump sum contract with a bill of quantities

The profit allowance is determined by the company's strategy, the market condition and the keenness in winning the job.

The allowance for overheads, risk and profit also depends on:

1. Does the contractor really want the job?
2. Economic climate. Is the construction industry booming?
3. Who are the competitors?
4. Is the project a prestigious one? If so, money is not the only factor.
5. Effect of joint venture partner, if any?
6. Any contractor's site nearby that can share some of the costs, especially the site on costs?

## 3.3    Writing up the Bill

The indirect cost and profit mark-up value may be shared and spread to all direct cost items to arrive at the tender total. The adjustment is known as 'rate loading' which is carried out when the total tender sum has been determined. This can be achieved by raising some of the bill items rate while the others are being lowered and keep the total tender sum the same. The objectives of 'rating loading' are:

1. To improve the cash flow for the project
2. To make extra money through adjustment due to price fluctuation
3. To make more profit on some items

The transfer of rates into the bill of quantities can be done manually by the estimator, followed by careful checking and then signed. The bill of quantities together with the appropriate documents such as tender programme are enclosed in a sealed envelope and submitted to the client on or before the closing date.

The process of finalizing a tender is shown in the flowchart in Fig. 5.6.

## 3.4    Additional Information to be Submitted With a Tender

### 3.4.1    Method Statement

It is essential that an early meeting be held between the estimator and the planning engineer to establish initial proposals relating to the method of construction. The following points are considered when deciding on the method of construction and resources to be used:

1. Site location, layout and access
2. Overlap of operations needed to meet programme requirements
3. Location and availability of labour and management within the company
4. Cost of recruiting additional labour
5. Availability of plant within and outside the company
6. Availability of materials, including long term delivery items
7. Current and future projects in the area which may affect the supply of basic resources
8. Quality of workmanship required
9. Special requirements of the project, such as special plant or skills needed
10. Amount of work to be subcontracted

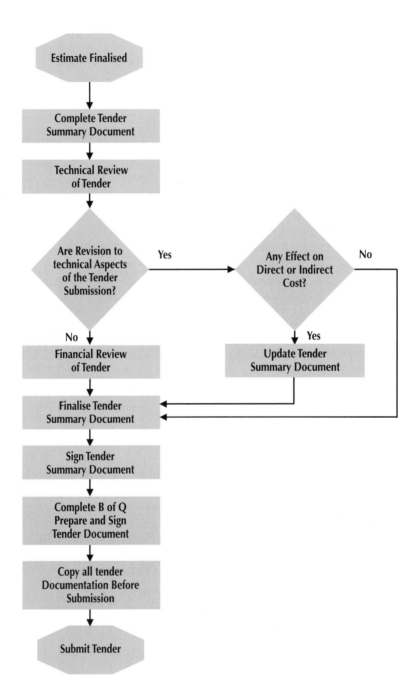

**Fig. 5.6**   Tender finalization.

11. Material handling on site including their storage, distribution and waste. The time span of the project and seasonal influences on method of construction and materials required.
12. Quality and complexity of the work.

The method statement outlines the sequence and method of construction upon which the estimate is based. It shows how the major elements of work will be handled and indicates areas where different methods will be used.

The main purposes of the method statement are:

1. To establish the principles on which the estimate is based
2. To announce the construction personnel of the resource limits which have been allowed in the estimate and to describe the method of working envisaged at the tender stage

### 3.4.2  Construction Programme

The planning techniques usually employed in the preparation of a construction programme are:

1. Bar charts

The bar chart can be presented in two forms. The first is the simple bar chart with a list of activities on the left and a time scale marked out from left to right. The start, duration and finish of each activity are represented by a bar. To create the chart, the planning engineer must list the activities and decide the start date, the duration and the interrelationship between the activities.

The second form is the linked bar chart, where the links or the dependencies between the activities are represented by vertical lines. This makes it clear which activities must be completed before the others can start.

2. Network analysis

The advantages of network planning are that the smaller self-contained steps used in creating the network and sequence of activities are indicated and that computers can be employed to aid the analysis.

The steps in producing a network are:

1. List all the activities involved
2. Produce a logic diagram, i.e. the sequence of each activity
3. Estimate the duration and calculate the start and finish times of each activity, and the float time available
4. Estimate the resources required by each activity

If the tender is successful, the programme prepared by the contractor represents the contractor's intention to carry out the construction work, the timing and the pricing.

### 3.4.3   Alternative Tender

In civil engineering and foundation construction contracts, it is usual to permit the submission of alternative designs with their prices. Alternative tenders should as far as practicable be encouraged as there may be a considerable advantage to the client in the alternative design, sequence and methods of construction offered by the tenderers, based on their experience in carrying out similar projects. An alternative tender generally consists of supporting information such as drawings, calculations and a priced bill of quantities addendum, so that its technical acceptability, construction time and economics can be fully assessed by the engineer.

## 3.5    Difficulties Encountered During the Tendering Period

The major difficulties encountered by the estimators for tendering are:

1.  Short period of time for preparing a tender
2.  The standard and incompleteness of contract documents
3.  Quantities measured by the engineer and his quantity surveyor are inaccurate
4.  Too many contract amendments by the engineer
5.  The clarity of specification requirements and the quality required
6.  Problems in coordination between partners in joint venture projects
7.  Risk factor is high due to too many uncertainties
8.  Limited source of cost data especially for new items of work
9.  Availability of competent and experienced subcontractors to submit quotations
10. Lump sum contracts would require the contractor to prepare the bill of quantities

All these difficulties will directly influence a contractor's bid price and eventually the tender sum will have to be adjusted.

### Acknowledgement

*Contributions from those contractors interviewed for a research on construction management practice and Mr H.M. Cheng's comments on this chapter are gratefully acknowledged.*

# 6

# RESOURCE MANAGEMENT AND PLANNING

## 1. Introduction

Resource management is an essential element in construction. The basic resources in construction are often called the four M's: Men, Machines, Material and Money. In this chapter, all these four resources are to be discussed.

Interviews with 15 large construction sites' managers in Hong Kong were conducted and their views on resource management are summarized in this chapter, with the exception of section 7, for which the number of interviewees was 20.

## 2. Manpower Management

### 2.1 Number of Labourers

The number of labourers in a construction project is found to increase with the increase of the following two indicators:

1. The contract sum
2. The S/D ratio (i.e. contract sum/project duration ratio)

The S/D ratio represents the speed of the programme of work. The higher the S/D ratio, the greater the number of labourers is on site.

## 2.2    Factors Affecting Labour

There are a number of factors which affect the decisions on the number and type of labour. They are listed in the order of decreasing importance as shown below.

1.   Programme of work
2.   Nature of work
3.   Subcontractors employed
4.   Overall cost
5.   Financial condition
6.   Location of site

The programme of work is found to be the most important factor. At the peak of the work programme, more labour would be employed, and vice versa. This finding can verify the finding in section 2.1 also. Other than the programme of work, the factors 'nature of work' and 'subcontractor employed' are also of considerable importance.

## 2.3    Subletting

Subletting works by the main contractor to subcontractors is a very common practice in Hong Kong. Over 90% of the labourers in a building site belong to subcontractor and only less than 10% belong to the main contractor. The situation is less extreme in a civil engineering construction site. About 75% of the labourers belong to subcontractors and 25% belong to the main contractor in the latter case. Such a phenomenon can be explained by the fact that the nature of work in buildings is too diversified and specialized. It is not economical for the main contractor to employ too much labour as the management cost would be increased. On the contrary, the works executed in civil engineering construction is relatively simple, and the contractors are more willing to employ their own labour who can do a wider range of jobs.

There are several factors which affect the decision of subletting. They are listed in the order of decreasing importance as shown below:

1.   Nature of work
2.   Cost consideration
3.   Operation of work

4.  Provision of labour
5.  Provision of plant

It is found that the nature of work mostly controls the decision on subletting. The main contractor often sublet such kinds of works which are too specialized. The cost is also an important consideration. It is often true that the cost in subletting is less than the cost incurred by the main contractor if the latter is carrying out the work himself because of the higher flexibility on the part of subcontractors.

The advantages of subletting works to subcontractors are:

1.  The main contractor finds it easier to control the cost of the works.
2.  The risks of works can be transferred from the main contractor to subcontractors.
3.  It is easier to control the allocation of resources, particularly equipment and plant.
4.  The productivity through subcontracting system is usually higher.

# 3    Plant Management

## 3.1    Factors Affecting Plant

The factors affecting the number and type of plant are listed in decreasing order of importance as shown below:

1.  Programme of work
2.  Nature of work
3.  Overall cost
4.  Limitations on site
5.  Self owned (stock of company)

The programme of work controls the number and the type of plant most of the time. The nature of work is also a crucial factor; different types of plant have different functions in executing works, especially for building works. Cost is also an important consideration. Moreover, the limitations on site also control the use of plant. For example, it is difficult to install a large plant on a small and congested site.

## 3.2    Ownership of Plant

The plant on site can be divided into self-owned or not self-owned by the main contractor. The latter can be further subdivided into hiring or subcontractors' provision. Tower cranes, material hoist and concrete pumps are usually owned by the main contractor. Mobile cranes, backhoe, bulldozer and rollers are usually not self-owned.

The factors affecting the ownership of plant are listed in decreasing order of importance as follows.

1.  Policy of company
2.  Further usage of plant
3.  Overall cost
4.  Duration of project
5.  Self-owned (stock of company)

Company policy is the most important factor in the ownership decision. This means that the decision is usually made at the contractor's head office where the management considers the total situation (i.e. other construction projects also) instead of a particular project.

## 4    Material Management

## 4.1    Ordering of Materials

Materials with a high and frequent demand throughout the construction period, such as ready-mixed concrete, are ordered directly on site. On the contrary, materials like sanitary fittings and waterproofing material are usually ordered through the head office because the quantity and the timing of their demand can be easily predicted. These are usually ordered in advance by one to several months. The ordering periods for materials ordered directly on site are much shorter of course, usually within days rather than months compared with head office ordering.

Because the working cycle for building projects is shorter than that for civil engineering projects, the average ordering period of materials in the former sites is significantly shorter than that in the latter sites.

## 4.2 Reordering

There are several factors affecting the frequency of reordering of materials. The most important factor is the progress of work. The frequency of reordering increases as the progress of work increases. The next important factor is the existing stock level. The third factor is the availability of storage area. For the third factor, it is less significant for civil engineering sites than building sites, as storage spaces are usually more readily available in the former case.

## 4.3 Storage

Besides ordering and reordering practices, a good storage practice on site is also important. Materials are mainly stored in storage rooms, covered storage yards and open air storage spaces. Fig. 6.1 shows how some common construction materials are stored in building sites. Fig. 6.2 shows the same in civil engineering sites.

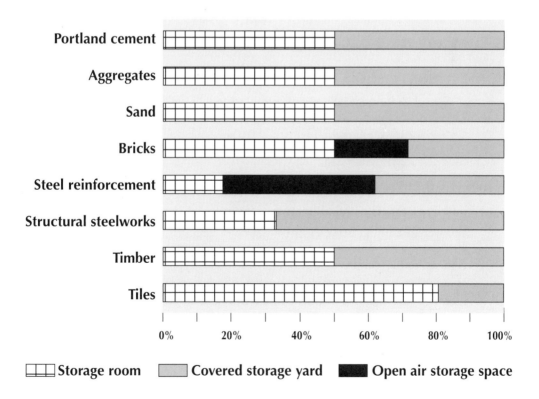

**Fig. 6.1**  Storage spaces for construction materials in building sites.

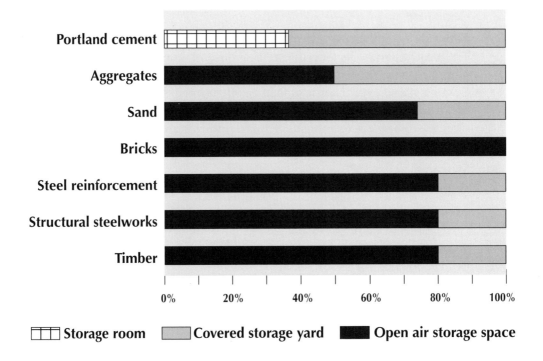

**Fig. 6.2** Storage spaces for construction materials in
civil engineering sites.

Usually, the open space of civil engineering sites is much more than that of building sites. The limitation on storage areas becomes less significant in the former sites and construction materials can be conveniently stored in open air storage areas. Furthermore, other than such common materials as concrete, cement, reinforcement and timber, some major types of materials in building and civil engineering construction are different. A large variation of types of materials are used in building sites. Such kinds of materials like sanitary fitting, electrical installations and finishing materials are expensive and easily damaged. It is therefore reasonable that materials for building sites are usually stored in storage rooms or covered storage yards.

## 5    Costs of Each type of Resources

### 5.1    Cost Proportions for Main Contractor

The total costs on a construction site mainly consist of labour cost, plant cost, material cost and overheads. The proportions of these costs for a main contractor are shown in Table 6.1.

| | Cost proportions for main contractor | |
| --- | --- | --- |
| | **Building work** | **Civil engineering work** |
| Labour | 9% | 26% |
| Plant | 21% | 14% |
| Materials | 35% | 32% |
| Overhead | 35% | 28% |

**Table 6.1**    Cost proportions of resources for a main contractor.

It can be observed that materials form the major cost for both building and civil engineering projects. The cost proportions for labour, however, are very different in building and civil works; the former is much lower than the latter. This is consistent with the finding in section 2.3 of this chapter, that is, the percentage of subletting in building works is higher than that in civil works. This means that the number of direct labourers of the main contractor is much lower in building works than in civil works. Because of the big difference in the labour cost, the overhead cost for civil works becomes lower than that for building works.

### 5.2    Cost Proportions for Subcontractor

On the contrary, the cost proportion of labour is much higher for subcontractors than for main contractors. Usually, subcontractors only provide labour and plant (and in some cases materials too) in construction processes. The need for administration and organization of works is not much compared with main contractors. Cost proportions for building main contractor and building subcontractors are shown in Table 6.2.

| Cost proportions (building works only) | | |
| --- | :---: | :---: |
| | **Main contractor** | **Subcontractor** |
| Labour | 9% | 33% |
| Plant | 21% | 28% |
| Materials | 35% | 34% |
| Overhead | 35% | 5% |

**Table 6.2**   Cost proportions of resources between main contractor and subcontractor.

Unfortunately, the same comparison for civil work main contractors and subcontractors could not be obtained in the interviews.

## 5.3   Cost Control

The measures for cost control of resources adopted on construction sites were also investigated. Fig. 6.3 shows the measures taken by main contractors to control costs. The use of bonus systems and the frequent check of stock of suppliers are the control measures adopted by less than half of the sites interviewed.

It can be seen that contractors in Hong Kong usually focus on control of daily work, particularly the regular checking and maintenance of plant and equipment as it is the contractors' responsibility by law. They do not seem to have enough concern about backup activities (e.g. bonus systems, checking of stock of suppliers, checking of quality of materials received). This might reflect the fact that construction management in Hong Kong has not yet attained the level of total quality management.

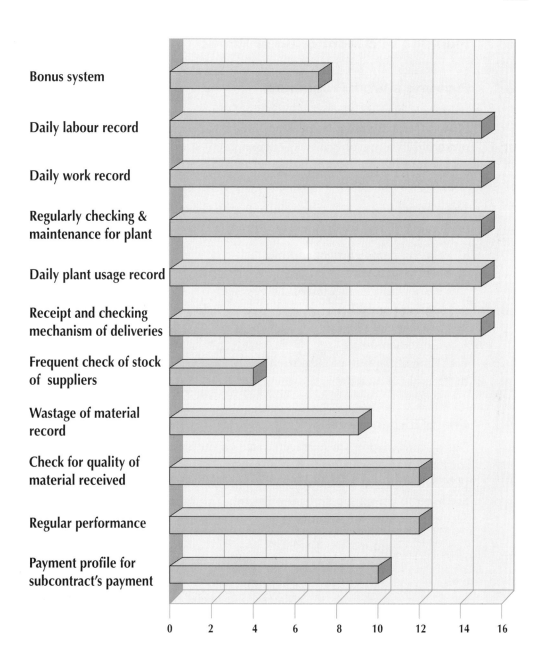

**Fig. 6.3**  Cost control measures for resources adopted on sites.

# 6    Planning and Monitoring of Works

## 6.1    Planning a Work Programme

In order to have an effective allocation of different kinds of resources, a good planning of work programme is important. A programme of work should be produced by a person with experience in construction processes and good understanding in the limitations due to resources, finance and client's requirement.

There are a number of factors which must be considered in planning a work programme. These factors are listed below in decreasing order of importance:

1. Date of completion of contract
2. Nature of work
3. Particular specification of the engineer
4. Labour force
5. Provision of plant
6. Limitation of site
7. Time of the year of construction
8. Supply of material

## 6.2    Charts for Monitoring

During construction, the managerial staff on site have to continuously monitor the execution of work so that a thorough comparison between the original plan (work programme) and the actual progress can be made. Usually, charts are used to act as tools of monitoring. The following lists these charts according to their importance:

Used most        ↑    Work progress chart
                        Financial progress chart
                        Manpower chart
                        Material usage chart
                        Plant usage chart
                        Cost of material usage chart
Used least        ↓    Subcontractor progress chart

It can be observed that the majority of contractors in Hong Kong apply monitoring charts of work progress and financial progress. It is rare to find monitoring charts of costs of materials and subletting schedule.

## 6.3    Method Statement

The preparation of method statements plays an important role on construction operations. The factors which are considered in drafting method statements are listed below in decreasing order of importance:

1.  Cost of work
2.  Safety consideration
3.  Limitation of site environment
4.  Programme of work
5.  Time required
6.  Experience on the work
7.  Demand of plant
8.  In-house technical support
9.  Demand of labour
10. Supply of materials

The general route from drafting to approving a method statement is as follows:

Draft by site engineer /planning engineer
↓
Discuss with subcontractor
↓
Coordinate with the site agent
↓
Endorsed by the contracts manager
↓
Submit by the engineer for approval

In general, the site agent usually has the power to make decisions as to construction operations. Such a kind of decision-making framework can eliminate the time for documentation and discussion between different departments in the head office. In other words, such a practice speeds up the progress of work when changes occur on site.

# 7    Subcontractor Management

In Hong Kong, subcontracting agreements are mostly confirmed in the form of formal letter of award. However, it still exists, in occasional circumstances, that the agreements be in the forms of endorsement on quotations or verbal confirmation. In this section, some important issues on subcontracting management are discussed.

## 7.1    Criteria for the Selection of Subcontractors

There are several criteria which affect the selection of subcontractors. They are listed in the order of decreasing importance as shown below:

1. Quality of work
2. Financial stability
3. Technical ability
4. Safety track record
5. Labour force stability
6. Management ability
7. Ability in meeting schedules
8. Work ethics

It is interesting to observe that the interviewees considered subcontractors' work ethics as a very low priority.

## 7.2    Criteria for the recruitment of new subcontractors

If a main contractor wishes to look for a new subcontractor, there are certain criteria for doing so. These criteria are listed in the order of decreasing importance as shown below:

1. Track records
2. Accumulated work experiences
3. Past client records
4. In-progress projects
5. Capital assets
6. Quality of human resources
7. Visit to subcontractor's factory

## 7.3   Problems and Difficulties Encountered With Subcontracting

Main contractors usually encounter problems/difficulties with subcontractors. The followings are the common problems/difficulties, shown in the order of decreasing importance:

1.   Quality of work
2.   Progress of work
3.   Lack of cooperation
4.   Difficulties in controlling
5.   Excess material wastage

## 7.4   *Suggestions for improvement of subcontractors*

Suggestions are given by the interviewees for improving the deployment of subcontractors in construction contracts. These suggestions are listed in the order of decreasing importance as shown below:

1.   Improvement on workers' skill
2.   Quality assurance improvement
3.   Improvement on labour supply stability
4.   Safety management improvement
5.   Improvement on method of work (method statement)
6.   Improvement on schedule control

Readers may observe that the points in section 7.3 are somehow related to those in this section. This is logical and reasonable.

# 7

# QUALITY MANAGEMENT

## 1. Introduction

The importance to contractors in getting their quality system certified to ISO 9000 is well known in the construction industry. Many clients, notably the Hong Kong SAR government departments, have made it a mandatory requirement for contractors intending to tender for projects under their administration and supervision. Since 1993, main contractors must attain the ISO 9000 certification for Hong Kong Housing Authority projects and it has been a trend for contracting firms to work towards the target of having their quality system accredited.

## 2. Meaning of Quality

Quality has different meanings depending on different organizations' perception and definition. In everyday use, the word quality usually carries implication of excellence, high status and sometimes deluxe feeling. BS 4778 defines quality as the totality of features and characteristics of a product and service that bears on its ability to satisfy the stated or implied needs. The German Standard, DIN, defines quality as all those properties and characteristics of a product or activity that affects its suitability to satisfy given requirements. Juran and Crosby, the quality gurus, consider quality as conformance to the given requirements. The former also believes that the quality must meet the test of its fitness for the intended use which seems to be in line with the conventional approach in controlling quality in construction.

## 2.1   Quality Control (QC)

Based on checking and inspection to ensure compliance with given specifications, quality control has long been used in construction. The essentials of quality control are to detect changes in quality by inspection and testing, and to make necessary adjustments to the production process. It provides useful feedback and enables defective areas to be given early attention or to be corrected. However, there have been numerous cases where ways were found to deceive or bypass the inspection. Since correction of substandard work causes delay, losses and pain to parties concerned, more frequent and stringent testings are often required.

## 2.2   Quality Assurance (QA)

Quality assurance embraces all the activities and functions needed to provide adequate confidence in a product or service for satisfying given requirements for quality. It is essentially a preventive function. Quality assurance is based on the principle that prevention is better than cure and it is more economical to get things right in the first place. Everyone should aim at doing things right the first time and every time, thus achieving zero defect in performance. To implement quality assurance, proper and systematic procedures are drawn up and followed by all concerned.

## 2.3   Differences Between QC and QA

While quality control is taken as a system of activities intended to provide a quality product, quality assurance is a planned system to ensure that the quality control programme is actually effective.

Quality control comprises those quality assurance actions related to the actual physical characteristics of the product, the hardware or the activity. Quality assurance includes and is broader than quality control. It is concerned with all the activities from initial conception through detailed design, manufacture, assembly etc., until the finished product is put into use.

## 3.    Quality Movement in the Hong Kong Construction Industry

Contractors in Hong Kong have long been concerned with quality and quality standards in meeting clients' requirements. Before 1990 quality of construction works was largely based on the first and second party assessment (Ahmed et al. 1998). These assessments were basically conducted through internal and external quality control activities such as checking and testing the completed works during different stages of construction processes. Such quality control activities were carried out in two phases. First, the contractor carried out the quality control in accordance with the requirements as stated in contract documents. Then the client's representative would check the quality of such works against the specifications and drawings.

In the 1960s, there was a great demand for public housing to accommodate new immigrants. A large quantity of public housing was built at that time, but much of it had been done at the expense of quality. The poor construction quality had led to the premature redevelopment of 26 housing blocks in 1986. As a result, the government realized the shortcomings of the traditional quality management based on the quality control approach in construction and recognized the quality assurance concept of getting it right the first time (Kam & Tang 1997).

In March 1990, the Hong Kong government launched a Quality Awareness Campaign and introduced the concept of quality management to Hong Kong (Tam 1996). The campaign had brought about a demand from clients for a quality assurance element in the products of service provided to them. Along with the government's campaign, the Hong Kong Housing Authority had taken three initiatives to strive for an improvement in the quality standards of its contractors. First, in January 1991, a Performance Assessment Scoring System scheme was proposed, which aimed at linking tendering opportunities with contractor's quality performance and capabilities. Then a Maintenance Assessment Scoring System scheme for maintenance works was proposed in 1991. In March 1993, the Housing Authority required that only building contractors certified to ISO9000 standards are eligible to tender for the housing projects.

Meanwhile, the Hong Kong Government Works Bureau had taken similar initiatives to improve quality management for public projects. Since April 1996, all engineering, architectural and associated consultants are required to be ISO9000 certified. Likewise, all Group C contractors (List I and List II) and specialist contractors for land piling are required to obtain ISO 9000 certification, effective from October 1996 and January 1998 respectively.

## 4. Quality Management System Standards

The International Organization for Standardization (ISO) adopted the ISO 9000 series as the standards for quality management systems. ISO Standards originated from the manufacturing industry where the abundance of processes that are required to produce a product makes it difficult to ensure quality. An obvious solution was to standardize the processes. Over time, each process was documented in detail and great efforts were made to ensure compliance.

The aim of the ISO series is to meet a conformance standard, rather than a performance standard. It depends on setting up some formal procedures and work instructions for employees to follow. All employees are expected to implement the adopted procedures to ensure that the work they perform is correct. External and internal inspections are carried out in order to investigate whether the procedures have been properly followed.

The ISO 9000 (1987) consists of the following:

ISO 9000 : Guidelines for selection and use of quality management and quality assurance standards
ISO 9001 : Model for quality assurance in design, development, production, installation and servicing
ISO 9002 : Model for quality assurance in production, installation and servicing
ISO 9003 : Model for quality assurance in final inspection and test
ISO 9004 : Guidelines for quality management and quality system elements

The ISO 9000 series serve to clarify the distinctions and interrelationships among the principal quality concepts. They provide guidelines for the selection and use of a series of international standards on quality systems for internal quality management purposes and external quality assurance purposes.

Lam et al. (1994) list the reasons of the popularity of using the Standards: The Standards are internationally recognized so everyone concerned can communicate on quality assurance using a common language. The series contains quality assurance criteria which are comprehensible and implementable, thus enabling firms to develop their quality systems. The Standards, facilitating third party auditing and certification on conformance to a recognized standard, undoubtedly provide confidence to customers (clients).

## 5.    Quality System Levels

There are different quality system levels, depending on the extent of rigour in carrying out the quality assurance and in determining the extent of application to elements of a quality assurance system. Quality system standards cover three levels of application.

### 5.1    Level 1: Design, Development, Production, Installation and Servicing (ISO 9001)

Level 1 is applied when the technical requirements of a product or service are specified principally in terms of the performance required, or where the design has not been established. Under such circumstances, the supplier is frequently responsible for the design, development, manufacture and field trials. Control of quality throughout all phases of this work is essential to ensure reliability and other characteristics.

### 5.2    Level 2: Production, Installation  and Servicing (ISO 9002)

Level 2 is applied when the technical requirements of products or service are specified in terms of established design, and where conformance to specified requirements can be ensured only by inspection and test during production.

### 5.3    Level 3: Final Inspection and Test (ISO 9003)

Level 3 is applied when conformance to specific requirements of products or services can be established by inspection and tests conducted on the finished product or service.

### 5.4    Applying the Clauses of ISO 9000

To establish a quality management system to meet the ISO 9000 standards, the contractor must address all the requirements stated in the respective standards. Although the standards were originated from the manufacturing industry, the requirements can be applied specifically to construction firm operations. As far as possible, the quality management system should be built on existing procedures and operating systems.

The elements of a quality assurance standard should not be confined to proof or evidence; they should also highlight activities which can minimize the risk of defective work at every stage of a process including its design, procurement and installation.

The following illustrates briefly the application of clauses of ISO 9000 to construction works:

1.  **Quality system:** requirements to set up, document and maintain a quality system

2.  **Organization:** delineation of responsibility as defined in the quality manual

3.  **Review of the quality system:** ensuring effectiveness of the quality system and its suitability to other projects

4.  **Planning:** e.g. logistics of constructing a basement wall

5.  **Work instructions:** for activities which affect quality such as batching of concrete

6.  **Records:** developing and maintaining a system of records for inspection by clients and as proof of quality assurance

7.  **Corrective action:** procedures to deal with dimensional discrepancy

8.  **Design control:** following a design standard, code of practice or in-house guidelines

9.  **Documentation and change control:** issuing and recording amended drawings

10. **Control of inspection, measuring and test equipment:** checking accuracy of steel bar testing machine

11. **Control of purchased material and services:** control of material suppliers and nominated subcontractor services

12. **Manufacturing control:** control of concreting operation on site

13. **Purchaser supplied material:** control of material and components supplied by the client

14. **Completed item inspection and test:** inspection and water test of the pipeline laid

15. **Sampling procedures:** procedures for sampling of concrete for tests

16. **Control of non-conforming material:** rejecting substandard bored pile or assigning a lower working load.

17. **Indication of inspection status:** identifying the inspected and approved formwork and reinforcement ready for concreting

18. **Protection and preservation of product quality:** covering the concrete surface for curing purpose

20. **Training:** identifying all training requirements for activities and functions which can affect quality

## 6.  ISO 9000: 2000 Version

The 1994 versions of the ISO 9000 family have been revised by ISO/TC176 for publication in December 2000. The scope of the standard has been enhanced. ISO 9001: 1994 uses the term 'quality assurance' and approaches quality assurance by preventing nonconformity. On the contrary, ISO 9001: 2000 uses the term 'quality management' and emphasizes the following requirements, including meeting customer requirements, meeting regulatory requirements, continual improvement and prevention of nonconformity of a quality management system

There are fundamental changes to the standard which include, inter alia, increased focus on top management commitment, the process approach to quality management, and the move beyond 'compliance' towards 'customer satisfaction' and 'continual improvement' (Lau 2001). Continual improvement is the process focused on continually increasing the effectiveness and efficiency of the organization to fulfill its policy and objectives. It ensures a dynamic evaluation of the quality management system and responds to the growing needs and expectations of customers.

One objective of ISO 9000: 2000 standards is to simplify the structure and reduce the number of standards within the family. This has been achieved by the following.

- The merging of ISO 9001: 1994, ISO 9002: 1994 and ISO 9003: 1994 by a single quality management system requirements standard, ISO 9001: 2000.
- The merging of ISO 8402 and part of the content of ISO 90000-1 into a new ISO 9000 standard, which is about fundamentals and vocabulary.
- The revision of ISO 9004-1 into a new ISO 9004 standard that provides supplementary guidelines to the new ISO 9001 standard.

The ISO 9000: 2000 series is based on eight quality management principles which are derived from the collective experience and knowledge of the internal experts who participated in ISO/TC 176. The principles are intended for use by senior management as a framework to guide their organizations towards improved performance. These eight principles include customer focused organization, leadership, involvement of people, process approach, system approach to management, continual improvement factual approach to decision making and mutually beneficial supplier relationship, which are contained in the ISO 9004: 2000 document.

The ISO 9001: 2000 introduced a major change to the structure of the standard, by re-grouping the Clauses 4.1 to 4.20 of the 1994 edition into four sections:

- Section 5 - Management responsibility
- Section 6 - Resource management
- Section 7 - Product realization
- Section 8 - Measurement, analysis and improvement

The topics of other sections are:

- Section 1 - Scope of the standard
- Section 2 - Normative reference
- Section 3 - Definition of terms
- Section 4 - General and documentation requirements of the quality management system

It can be seen that the contents of the standard are now organized into a more systematic and readable manner.

The revised ISO 9001: 2000 and ISO 9004: 2000 standards were developed as a 'consistent pair' of standards. The former addresses more clearly the quality management system requirements for an organization has to demonstrate its capability to meet customer needs, whereas the latter is intended to lead beyond ISO 9001 towards the development of a comprehensive quality management system, designed to address the needs of all interested parties. Together, the primary aim of the consistent pair is to apply a modern quality management into the processes and activities of an organization, including promotion of continual improvement and achievement of customer satisfaction.

# 7.    Developing and Implementing a Quality System

## 7.1    Definitions (BS 4778)

### Quality system

The organization structures, responsibilities, activities, resources and events that together provide organized procedures and methods of implementation to ensure the capability of the organization to meet quality requirements. It is the management structure of an organization which relates to activities affecting the quality of the work being carried out.

### Quality manual

A document setting out the general quality policies, procedures and practices of an organization.

The quality manual should comprise the following:

1.    Company policy statement which includes a statement, a summary of activities undertaken and the firm's policy objectives towards implementing a quality system in accordance with the requirements of a standard.
2.    General statement to amplify the company's commitment to implementing a quality system.
3.    Amendment re-issue and distribution.
4.    Authority and responsibility included in the firm's organization.
5.    Summary of different procedures.

### Quality procedures

These are documents describing the activities involved in conducting business which are essential to the achievement of quality, e.g. instructions for the production of concrete would require a quality procedure. They are in fact method statements which make reference to relevant specification documents.

The quality procedures should include:

1.    Scope and purpose of the procedures
2.    Sequence of actions
3.    Persons responsible in the execution and for ensuring the requirement is met
4.    Remedial actions if non-conformance is detected

In preparing the quality procedures, the construction firm has already had a number of in-house procedures in controlling its work. Therefore, a substantial part of the preparation of the quality documents entails collecting, documenting and systematizing existing procedures, instructions and practices. The quality documents should be based on the existing practices, as long as they are in compliance with the established policies.

### Quality plan

This is the document derived from the quality system setting out the specific quality practices, resources and activities relevant to a particular contract or project. Normally a quality plan comprises an organization's quality manual, the relevant standard quality procedures and any additional specific quality procedures.

### Quality audit

This is the independent examination to monitor the effective implementation of a quality management system. Quality auditing can relate to the quality of a product, process or system. It is usually carried out on a periodic basis and involves independent and systematic examination of actions that influence quality. The objective is to ascertain that a quality system will comply with the contract requirements. Auditing a quality system is undertaken regularly to examine whether a quality system, quality plan or quality procedure is effective in achieving quality objectives.

The quality audit should be carried out by the personnel independent of the specific activities being audited and should cover:

1. Non-compliance or deficiencies with reasons
2. Suggestion on corrective actions
3. The implementation and effectiveness of corrective actions suggested in previous audits.

## 7.2    Developing a Quality System

The following are essential stages in developing and implementing a certified quality system.

### Stage 1

The chief executive of the firm should make a commitment to quality assurance by declaring a quality policy such as 'Towards total customer satisfaction' and making a formal statement of the objectives such as 'To achieve ISO 9002 certification in 18 months' time'. Organizing the management structure and defining responsibilities then follow.

### Stage 2

Examine and review the existing internal documentation, activities and procedures prior to preparation of quality manual and quality procedures, that is, the quality system.

### Stage 3

When the quality system is completed and fully approved internally, apply the general quality procedures to specific contracts. Staff should be familiar with quality assurance and understand their roles. However, training would be required.

### Stage 4

For specific contracts, the firm has to prepare quality plans and additional quality procedures.

### Stage 5

The quality plan is applied to the specific contract and further training may be necessary.

### Stage 6

Internal and external audit of the quality system are being implemented. All quality manuals and quality procedures should be reviewed periodically.

## 8.   Cost and Benefits of Quality Assurance

### 8.1   Cost

Quality cost consists of:

1. Cost of conformance — prevention cost and appraisal cost
2. Non-conformance cost

Cost of conformance includes prevention and appraisal costs. Prevention costs are required for actions taken to investigate, prevent or reduce defects or failures, and are spent to ensure things are right the first time. Appraisal costs are incurred in activities associated with assessment of the quality achieved, such as inspection, testing, internal audits, reviews etc. Costs of non-conformance (failure cost) are those required for rectifying everything discovered to be wrong.

An effective quality management system should lead to cost savings. However, it is not easy to find concrete evidence on the cost savings in construction. Literature and reports estimate that the cost of remedial work can be up to 15% of the building construction cost. A study (Burati et al. 1992) in the US suggested that as much as 12.4% of project cost was avoidable, and could be minimized by adopting quality assurance for the construction process. The two main causes of avoidable costs were:

1.  Design faults — 9.5% of project cost and was the most important cause of contract claims
2.  Construction faults — 2.5% of project cost.

Another study (Byrne 1993) of two local completed projects was undertaken by the Technical Audit Unit of the Works Branch. It was found that about 9% of total project cost was due to design error, change or omission.

The cost of setting up a quality assurance system was about $0.5 to 3 million, depending on the size of the contracting firm. The running cost can be up to 1% of the contract value with a mean of about 0.2% (Tam 1996).

## 8.2 Benefits

Many studies have suggested the following benefits for quality assurance implementation.

1.  Reduction in wastage
2.  Better team spirit
3.  Less staff conflict, enhanced job satisfaction
4.  Increased efficiency
5.  Confidence to clients, less customer complaints, lower rejection rates, less reworks
6.  Improved sales
7.  Shorter lead times
8.  Better relationship with subcontractors
9.  Reduced cost, increased profit

10. Improved systems and standardized procedures
11. Better workmanship, guaranteed quality

However, a survey (Tam 1996) on the actual benefits experienced by contractors indicated that they were not achieved as expected. Only the following have been reported with significant improvement:

1. Site control and condition
2. Overall quality awareness
3. Filing and documentation system leading to less reliance on memory, speedier information update
4. Delineation of responsibility
5. Competitiveness
6. Planning

Marginal improvements have been reported in:

1. Internal management
2. Site supervision and management
3. Staff morale and motivation

No improvement or doubts in improvement were observed in:

1. Safety and security
2. Reduction in defects, wastages, rework, and in project duration
3. Internal site communication
4. Coordination and communication with architect and consultant
5. Agreement on performance criteria with clients

## 9. Total Quality Management (TQM)

### 9.1 Definition and Meaning of TQM

In BS7850, TQM is defined as 'management philosophy and company practices that aim to harness the human and material resources of an organization in the most effective way to achieve the objectives of the organization'.

According to Nathan (1997), 'TQM is a holistic management philosophy that seeks continuously to maximize customer satisfaction, and continually to identify and eliminate non-value-adding activities from the organization.

TQM is not merely about implementing dynamic management systems; it is also about embedding a culture of continuous improvement and customer focus within an organization.'

The definition of TQM by the Department of Defense in USA (Tingey 1997) is 'a philosophy and a set of guiding principles that represent the foundation of a continuously improving organization. TQM is the application of quantitative methods and human resources to improve the material and services supplied to an organization, all the processes within the organization, and the degree to which the needs of the customer are met, now and in the future. TQM integrates fundamental management techniques, existing improvement efforts, and technical tools under a disciplined approach focused on continual improvement.'

From the above definitions, TQM philosophy is composed of total participation, continual improvement and customer focus. Thus, TQM can be regarded as a management-led process to obtain the involvement of all employees, in the continuous improvement of the performance of all activities, as part of normal business to meet the needs and satisfaction of both the internal and external customer. The principal benefit of commencing a TQM programme is to obtain and improve the future health of the business.

The importance of TQM was highlighted from a research study (Burati et al. 1992) on the construction industry in the US. It was suggested that 'Companies which do not implement TQM in their firms will not be competitive in the national and international construction market within the next five to ten years.'

TQM in construction is achieved by ensuring that the right attitude exists throughout the project and across company boundaries. All those involved — such as the client, designer, contractor and subcontractor — have a part to play and all must be committed to the common goal of total quality in construction.

The European Construction Institute (1993) recommends that the following objectives are to be achieved in order to attain total quality in construction:

C - Commitment by top management
O - Organization and structure for total quality management
N - Normal financial control
S - Supplier relationships
T - Training, education and safety awareness

R - Relationships with customers
U - Understanding and commitment by employees
C - Communications
T - Teamwork
I - Independent certification to ISO 9000
O - Objective measurement
N - Natural use of tools and techniques

The principle for adopting TQM is to stay in business. There is a need to continually improve everything we do and TQM provides the vehicle for achieving this. Applying these concepts will help:

1.  Improve the bottom line — Reduce rework and remove unnecessary procedures.
2.  Delight the client — Improve efficiency of the contractor and give results both the client and the contractor would benefit.
3.  Involve all the workforce — The workforce will feel more involved, realize their opinion counts and be able to contribute ideas to make the project a success.

There is an argument that the construction industry is highly organized around finite individual projects, so it may be impossible to apply principles of continuous improvement. However, assuming the contracting parties are pursuing a total quality process within their companies, it is possible to treat each project as an opportunity for quality improvement teams to address the improvement of some aspects of quality performance. Individuals who have experienced quality management activity on one project are then able to carry their experience forward beneficially to their next project, provided that the industry and the contracting parties are encouraging the process.

## 9.2 Differences Between QA and TQM

Quality assurance is a systematic approach in satisfying given requirements and providing adequate confidence, which is only part of total quality management. Total quality management provides the principles, tools and techniques to satisfy customers, both internal and external. It is a process to obtain continuous improvement of the performance of all activities. Rework, scrap, delivery delays, etc. may be minimized by adopting QA. However, other, largely hidden defects — such as unnoticed delays, frustration, redundant internal effort, over control, manpower inefficiency, and low morale — can only be exposed and cured by adopting TQM.

The European Construction Institute (1993) identifies the following differences between QA and TQM:

| Quality Assurance | Total Quality Management |
|---|---|
| 1. A part of the quality improvement process | A process for continuous improvement |
| 2. A systematic approach to influence attitudes and working environment | Change in attitudes and the working environment to provide tools, techniques and systems for continuous improvement |
| 3. Aims to ensure customers requirements are met every time | Creates a right first time attitude to delight the customers |
| 4. Provides a baseline for measuring the cost of quality | Recognizes cost of quality as vital and provides measurement for continuous improvement |
| 5. Provides confidence to the customer of the quality of the product or service | Enables customers and employees to recognize the supplier of the product or service as a quality company |
| 6. Provides the means to reduce waste | Seeks to eliminate waste |
| 7. Enhances publicity and image | Attracts publicity and the company is used as a role model for quality |
| 8. Provides procedures for doing things right | Provides for doing the right things right |
| 9. Make improvements by eliminating recurring problems | Make improvement by cultural change based on measurement of performance and elimination of root causes and constraints |

| | |
|---|---|
| 10. Requires a structured organization and a statement of key responsibilities | Creates a culture in the organization that seeks to continuously improve in all its activities |
| 11. Provides, as a directive, procedures for all activities and working procedures | Focuses on a full understanding of the various business processes by day to day involvement of all concerned |
| 12. Provides quality records of all activities | Uses quality records for measurement and for continuous improvement |
| 13. Relies on regular monitoring and audits to identify and correct non-conformance | Involves getting ideas and suggestions for improvements from everyone |
| 14. Uses regular management reviews of the procedures and working practices to lead to improvement | Stresses the importance that products and services delivered to the internal and external customer will meet requirements whether specified or not |
| 15. Ensures that people are trained and experienced | Ensures that everybody in the organization receives education and training to enable them to do their job effectively and achieve personal satisfaction |

In order to control the work processes such as recognizing the problems including tracing their root causes and implementing effective remedies, TQM requires the use of the following tools and techniques (European Construction Institute 1993):

1. Histograms and scatter diagrams to gather and display data
2. Brainstorming to encourage creative thinking and generation of ideas
3. Matrix analysis in shortlisting and ranking using a two-dimensional matrix
4. Paired comparisons in prioritizing and ranking a number of alternatives to achieve a specified criteria (analytic hierarchy process)
5. Ranking and rating in placing the options in order of preference by using a score system
6. Pareto analysis to separate the major causes of the problems from the minorones
7. Cause and effect diagrams, such as the fish bone diagram, to identify potential causes of a problem
8. Failure prevention analysis to anticipate problems before they happen
9. Force and field analysis to identify the forces that help or obstruct a change
10. Process flow chart to show the sequence and resources of the activities

## 10.    *Effectiveness in Implementing Quality Assurance System*

ISO 9000 requires standardized and systematic production procedures. It emphases documentation control which covers day-to-day management, production and administrative activities. A certified QA system clearly shows the objective, evidence and traceability. The success of developing and implementing a certified quality system relies on commitment and encouragement of top management, and the support and participation of staff.

It can be seen that the ISO 9000 series would be very appropriate to large firms with well defined organization structure and established procedures. A survey (Poon and Xu 1997) indicated that 80.3% of large construction firms in Hong Kong have been certified to ISO 9000, while only 5.3% and 31.4% of small and medium size firms have their quality systems being accredited.

The low percentage of small to medium size contractors with certified QA systems was due to the client's low priority on quality, the difficulty to adjust the management style by owners of typical Chinese family business, and the resistance to change by their staff.

Another study (Tam 1996) on the effectiveness of the QA system in the Hong Kong construction industry concluded that the benefits of QA schemes previously claimed were based on no strong evidence. Contractors considered the certification exercise as a means of securing inclusion of their firms on the lists of tenderers. Their commitment to quality was not genuine.

Ahmed et al. (1998) identified that benefits of ISO certification such as 'improved profitability, effectiveness and efficiency' and 'reduced cost of correcting errors' were not significant and below the original expectations. Even some certified construction companies considered ISO 9000 quality system was not suitable for them and the reasons were 'too much paper work', 'culture of workers in Hong Kong' and 'insufficient training provided'.

According to Ahmed's study, the most common reason for the contractor to seek certification was the statutory requirement by the government. The ISO certificate becomes a 'work permit' and no contractor can afford to ignore it. The study also revealed that the overall benefits, which contractors have gained as a result of implementing a Quality Management System (QMS) to ISO 9000, have not been significant. Respondents indicated that the level of improvement was below their original expectations. Many contractors seek ISO 9000 certification due to pressure from clients, and they fail to reap the benefits because of the wrong attitude in implementing the QMS.

A similar survey by Tang and Kam (1999) for ISO 9000 certified engineering consultants in Hong Kong showed that government requirement was the prime reason for seeking certification. It also indicated that the actual achievements and overall benefits which the consultants have gained as a result of implementing a QMS to ISO 9001 were not significant and below original expectations. The authors considered that ISO 9001 standard was the foundation of TQM. Moreover, it was hoped that the consulting engineering firms would take ISO 9001 as a stepping stone to total quality management.

Surveys (Au 2000; Lee 1997; Kam and Tang 1998) indicated that the majority of construction firms were under pressure from clients, and the firms that were passive in adopting ISO9000 reaped less benefits from implementing the system. There was no clear and objective mechanism in linking the contractors' past quality performance to the current tender assessment. The final outcome is still likely to be the 'lowest bid policy' for a group of tenders which have already met the set minimum requirements. This tends to convey a message to the local contractors that, once they have achieved the ISO 9000 certification status for tendering, their chance to win a contract still relies on the competition on price. The survey (Lee 1997) also identified that a large proportion of the ISO 9000 certified firms tended to continue their pursuit of quality and management after being certified to ISO 9000.

In the UK, an investigation confirmed that the emphasis of management quality systems was on controlling operative performance by trying to detect defects through checking, rather than by managing in such a way as to prevent defects. The existing approach was thus ineffective.

The above were attempts to explain the reasons of deficiency and ineffectiveness in implementing QA systems. There is, thus, a strong need of promoting TQM in order to cure the quality problem genuinely.

# 8

# SAFETY MANAGEMENT

## 1. Introduction

Hong Kong's construction industry has a very poor safety track record as compared with other countries such as Japan, Singapore and England. The number of industrial accidents in construction, as one of the major economic sectors in Hong Kong, was 9,206 in year 2001, according to the 2001 Report of the Commissioner for Labour.

## 2. Major Attributes to Construction Accidents

There is usually more than one attribute to a particular construction accident on site. In most cases, it is a combination of various attributes, which may include negligence of construction workers, insufficient guidance and supervision by supervisory staff, inadequate financial, technical and moral support from senior management, untidiness on site, poor coordination between sub-contractors, and design faults.

A report published by the International Labour Office (ILO) in 1995 had the following comments on the safety record for the Hong Kong construction industry:

In 1991, 374 reportable accidents per 1,000 workers were recorded. This figure is approximately twice that of the United States and 25 times worse than Japan and Singapore (Lingard and Rowlinson, 1994). United Kingdom figures show that approximately three construction workers in every 1,000 suffer a major injury each year. The equivalent figure for Hong Kong in 1990 was 66 per 1,000 (ibid.). The problem is not, of course, confined to migrant workers, but the high proportion of recent immigrants from China in the workforce is an important factor - as is the extensive use of casual labour and subcontracting, traditional construction methods (including bamboo scaffolding), low expenditure on safety on the part of contractors and poor enforcement of existing safety legislation (ibid.). (International Labour Office, 1995: 88-89)

In addition, the following local practice and construction conditions also adversely affect construction safety in Hong Kong.

## 2.1    Procurement Method

The most common form of procurement method for construction work in Hong Kong is by the use of 'traditional method' (i.e. selective competitive tendering). With this traditional method, tenderers are firstly short-listed by the developer based on their working experiences, track records, and business relationship with that developer. Selected tenderers are invited to tender for the construction work. However, the final selection of the successful tenderer for the job is mainly based on the tendering price, and the contract is usually awarded to the tenderer who had submitted the lowest bid. Little consideration is given to safety measures provided by the tenderer, or the tenderer's safety record. Thus, there is no motivation for contractors to perform better in terms of construction safety in order to improve their chances of securing more jobs in future. Stronger emphasis should be placed on safety performance in the process of selecting an appropriate contractor for construction works.

## 2.2    Multi-layers of Sub-contracting

Sub-contracting is a very common practice in the local construction industry. It is not uncommon for a construction project to have more than 50 sub-contractors on site, with more than 80% of work in terms of contract sum to be sub-contracted. Laying and curing of concrete, bending and fixing of steel reinforcement bar, erection of timber formwork, and installation of electrical and mechanical plants, etc., are all common construction trades for sub-contracting purposes. The use of excessive sub-contracting practice will adversely affect the efficiency and effectiveness of communication of safety-related information and coordination of site activities, which may lead to construction accidents due to poor coordination, lack of proper instructions, and misunderstanding between working trades.

## 2.3  Working Conditions

Workers in Hong Kong usually have to work long hours. They work for an average of 48 hours per week in the fourth quarter of 1999, as compared with an average of 40 hours per week for most workers in developed countries.

## 2.4  Weather and Out Door Activities

Study in the past had indicated that the high accident rate during the summer in Hong Kong coincided with high level of rainfall and temperature in that period of year.

By average, June, July and August are the months when the number of hand-dug caisson accidents is at the highest. However, statistics indicated that June, July and August are not the months when there are more caisson construction activities. One of the possible explanations is the effect of the rainy season during these months, which may create more difficult working conditions on site. Another reason may be the hot-humid weather and high temperate which may cause fatigue much more easily amongst workers on an open site (Wong 1987).

## 2.5  Hazardous Operations

There are many hazardous operations for construction works on site. Some operations, such as hand-dug caisson, are so dangerous that the Works Bureau and the Hong Kong Housing Authority have issued practice notes to structural engineers and architects, forbidding the use of hand-dug caisson for foundation and slope protection purposes, unless special permission is given by the authorities.

A research has indicated that the major safety problems for hand-dug caisson are associated with the use of equipment including electrical chain-block, bucket, steel hook, and safety catch:

The main categories of fatal hand-dug caisson accidents are 'Fall of Person' and 'Falling Objects'. More emphasis should be put on the safe use of the bucket, and particularly, the proper functioning of the hooks and safety catches. Better design for a more robust and heavy-duty safety catch should be adopted to prevent any detachment from the hook.

Bucket used to lift workers should be at least 1m in depth and the passenger should stand inside the bucket. Heavy penalties should be imposed on all offenders including both the Main Contractor and the individuals (Wong 1987).

## 2.6    High Risk Acceptance and Ignorance of Risk

The public in general believes that construction involves dangerous activities and accept that it is impossible to meet all safety requirements in construction works. The fact that numerous parties participate in a contract also leads to the passing of responsibility for an accident from one party to another.

People who accept the risk of accidents without taking any further action are usually the result of ignorance. There are a number of reasons for this including group pressure, stubbornness and resistance to change. Once an accident has occurred, the attitude of most people concerned may change, but that may be too late and too costly.

## 2.7    Poor Housekeeping

All access or passageway should be properly maintained and clear of obstruction or unstable stacking. Poor housekeeping not only creates accidents but also causes danger to others in times of emergency.

## 3.    Safety System

To make significant improvements in construction safety, it is essential for all contractors, both large and small, to establish and implement a comprehensive safety system in their company and on sites. It is also a legal requirement as stipulated by the Factories and Industrial Undertakings (Safety Management) Regulation. Under this regulation, proprietors and contractors have the duties to develop, implement and maintain a safety management system, to prepare a written safety policy, and to establish a safety committee in their industrial undertakings. In general, there are 15 major items to be considered in a safety system.

## 3.1 Written Safety Policy

The top management of an organization should formulate its own safety policy. The safety policy should be in writing, and preferably in both Chinese and English. It should clearly spell out the commitment of the company towards construction safety.

Either the Chairman or the Chief Executive Officer of the company should sign the company's safety policy. Copies of company safety policy should be kept in the site office and posted at a noticeable location on site so that site staff can refer to it easily. It should be used as a reference, not only to supervisory staff, but also to workers and operatives. The main contractor's safety policy should also be included in all sub-contract documents for all sub-contractors' reference and for their workers to follow. Nowadays, many clients require contractors to submit their company safety policies together with their tender documents at the tendering stage.

The main function of a company safety policy is to state clearly the position and commitment of the senior management of a particular company towards good safety practice on site. Also, it is useful to provide sufficient guidance and directions for the establishment of company safety system in the long run.

## 3.2 Formal Safety Organization Structure

Contractors should have a clear safety organization structure in the form of an organization chart. The chart should be displayed at a noticeable location in the head office for easy reference. It should clearly state the structure of the safety organization and specify the roles and responsibilities of all the concerned parties, e.g. safety department, as well as personnel such as safety manager.

## 3.3 Safety Manual

A set of comprehensive safety manual for a particular project should be kept on site. It should be readily available to all site staff for reference, or for use in case of emergency. Information to be included in the safety manual is as follows:

1. The exact title, site address, lot number, and location map for the project.
2. The names, contact telephone numbers and addresses for the client, the architect, and the consultants.

3. The telephone numbers and addresses of the nearby police station, fire station and hospital.
4. The telephone numbers and addresses of the district offices for the relevant government departments, such as the Labour Department, Drainage Services Department, and Buildings Department.
5. The contact telephone numbers and pager numbers of the site project manager, the site engineers, and the safety officer.
6. Safety organization structure in the form of an organization chart or sketch, with names and positions of all those concerned staff.
7. Emergency procedures.

Standard procedures for events such as accident, out-break of fire, typhoon, flooding, and leakage of dangerous chemicals should be presented in writing and in logical sequences in the safety manual.

## 3.4    Accident Reporting Procedures

1. Factories and Industrial Undertaking Regulations Clause No.17 requires contractor's representative on site to report all accidents with severe injury or death as a result, to the Employees' Compensation Section of the Labour Department within 24 hours.
2. If the injured person is dead as a result of an accident, the contractor has to report the incident to the Factory Inspectorate Division of the Labour Department within 24 hours.
3. The contractor has to report to the nearest police station, either verbally or in writing, concerning the death of a worker due to an accident on site.
4. If an injured worker who has been certified by a medical doctor to be off work for three days or more, the contractor has to submit Form 2 to the Labour Department within seven days.
5. In the report submitted to the Labour Department, the following information should be included:

- Employers' particulars
- Particulars of the injured or deceased worker, including name, address, sex, age, and identity card number
- Date, condition and causes of the accident happened
- Conditions of injury
- Statement whether the injury or death was directly caused by the accident

## 3.5 Safety Committee at Company Level

A company safety committee is responsible for the maintenance and up-keeping of the overall company safety standard, whereas a safety committee at project level (i.e. site level) is responsible for the implementation of company safety policy and safety system for a specific project on site.

Company safety committee meetings should be held at least once every two months. A member of senior management, such as the chairman or CEO of the company, should chair the meeting. It should be attended by the safety manager of the company, and all the safety officers on site. Safety officers have to give both written and verbal report on the safety conditions of all the projects in hand. The main objectives of the company safety committee meeting are:

1. To formulate safety policy and safety system, which are applicable for all construction projects.
2. To provide back-up services to site safety committee, and to give advice to individual site safety committee in terms of:
   • Use of special safety equipment
   • Claim and compensation matters for injury resulted from accidents on site.
   • Safety and legal matters for the information of site project managers and site safety committees.
3. To monitor the latest development in safety related legislation and to inform site staff accordingly.
4. To receive and to vet safety reports submitted by site safety committees.
5. To compile and provide information generated from accident statistical analysis.

## 3.6 Safety Committee at Project Level

A site safety committee should be established for every construction site. Safety committee meetings are to be held on site, either on a weekly or biweekly basis. The main objective of having site safety committee meetings is to review the overall site safety conditions, and if necessary, to rectify site operational procedures in order to improve safety.

People who should participate in site safety committee include the project manager, safety officers, safety supervisors, foremen, and representatives from subcontractors.

### 3.7   Safety Training Scheme

Safety training schemes are to be provided to employees at different rankings and levels, including site management staff, workers and operatives of different trades. All safety training courses should be organized in such a way that they will not directly affect the normal progress of work on site.

Staff who have completed a training course should be issued with a certificate, as a kind of encouragement and for record purposes.

### 3.8   Safety Equipment

General safety equipment include safety helmet, safety glove, safety boot, safety belt, and safety goggles. All safety equipment should be provided by contractors to their workers free of charge. Other special safety equipment such as respiration apparatus for working in confined spaces (such as tunneling work) should be provided according to the legislative requirements as stipulated by the Factories and Industrial Undertakings (Confined Space) Regulation.

### 3.9   Safety Promotion

Contractors should organize in-house safety promotion activities and participate in public safety promotion campaigns organized by bodies such as the Hong Kong Construction Association Limited (HKCA) or the Occupational Safety and Health Council (OSHC). Participation in these schemes improve the safety awareness of both supervisory staff and workers. Also, comparison can be made in terms of the level of safety performance between contractors. As such, contractors can understand the industrial norm of safety performance, and be aware of their relative safety performance levels as compared with their counterparts.

### 3.10   Safety Checklist

Contractors should issue a standardized safety checklist for the use of safety officers and safety supervisors for site safety inspection purposes so that they can carry out their inspection more efficiently. Also, a record of safety inspection using the standardized checklist can be maintained for future reference.

Scores or grading should be allocated to items in the safety checklist. For example, a three level grading system may be adopted to indicate the degree of priority, and whether or not immediate remedial action is needed. Grade

A represents 'Adequate', Grade B represents 'Improvement is needed', and Grade C represents 'Immediate Action'. Items that may be included in the checklist are:

1. Site layout
   - site hoarding and covered walkway
   - site fence and main entrance
   - internal transit and drive way
2. Excavation work
   - shoring and support
   - ladder and other access
   - safety barrier
3. Working platform
   - base plate and ground support
   - vertical, lateral and diagonal supports
   - safety railing and toe boards
4. Ladder
   - location of steel ladder - away from high voltage over-head cable
   - securing the top portion of ladder - to prevent side-way movement
   - positioning of the top portion of ladder - at least 1 m above landing of the working platform
5. Structural steel installation
   - provision of working platform
   - fixing points for safety belt
   - safety net
6. Demolition
   - reference to structural drawings and as-built drawings
   - provision of working platform
   - removal of debris to prevent overloading
7. Work in confined space
   - sufficient supply of fresh air / removal of toxic gases
   - availability of respiration apparatus / life-line
   - continuous monitoring by co-workers outside the confined working space
8. Transportation
   - inspection and maintenance of transportation vehicles
   - competent and qualified operatives
   - reverse signaling and banks-man

9.  Tower crane / mobile crane
    - inspection and testing certificate
    - weekly inspection and inspection report
    - indication of loading and handling distance
10. Fire prevention
    - fire extinguisher
    - unobstructed access and egress
    - storage for inflammable goods

## 3.11   Safety Inspection

Site inspection should be carried out by safety officers and safety supervisors on a daily basis to ensure that safety procedures for construction operations are adhered to and safety measures are adopted by workers. Either verbal or written warning should be given to any non-compliance of safety procedures and measures. The safety personnel may even request the site project manager to order a construction operation to stop, if it is likely that the continuation of that particular operation may lead to an accident or mishap on site.

## 3.12   Safety Audit / Safety Review

According to the Factories and Industrial Undertakings (Safety Management) Regulation, and depending on their sizes, contractors are now required to appoint either registered safety auditors to conduct safety audits, or safety review officers to conduct safety review, once every six months. The safety audit or review can identify the under-performed safety aspect of the company, thereby improving the average level of safety knowledge and safety awareness of its staff. As a result, the productivity as well as the safety reputation of the company can be up-graded.

## 3.13   Safety Records

Periodical safety records have to be prepared by safety officers on either a weekly or biweekly basis. Safety records should reflect the various stages of construction works on site in general, and specific hazardous construction operations, such as deep basement excavation and dismantling of scaffolding, in particular. The purpose of these safety records is to provide safety related information for the site project manager and his supervisory team to monitor production on site, and to take precautionary measures against the possible happening of accidents.

## 3.14  Accident Investigation and Report

All accidents and mishaps on site should be reported both internally to the company's safety committee by the use of the company's accident report, and externally to the Labour Department by the use of Form 2. Preliminary investigation should be carried out by the safety officer. Relevant information such as the date, time, location, trade, name of injury, type of operation, cause(s) of accident, etc. are to be included in the accident report. It is also very useful to include both photographs and sketches to indicate details of the accident in the investigation report.

An accident investigation should be conducted promptly after the accident, so that first-hand information and important data related to the causes of accident can be collected without delay. Methods of accident investigation can be classified as follows:

1.  Data collection and recording on the spot where the accident happened — Direct measurement and taking photographs.
2.  Interviews — Including the injured person, his co-workers and other workers on site.
3.  Scrutinizing contract documents and files — To trace data and information recorded before the accident happened on site.
4.  Observation on site — To study workers' behaviour and the sequence of works.
5.  Questionnaire — To obtain a greater number of collected data for analysis (more suitable for opinion survey, and gathering information on the perception of general safety matters).

## 3.15  Accident Statistical Analysis

The company's safety committee or safety department should be responsible for collection of information and analysis of accident statistical data. In addition, it should be responsible for recording the trend and number of accidents on a monthly, quarterly and annual basis. Also, it should record the trend of accidents classified by the nature of works such as new build, maintenance, demolition, building and civil engineering. With a better understanding of the correlation between the number of accidents and the nature of works, more appropriate measures can be adopted to effectively reduce the occurrence of accidents on site.

## 4.    Related Organizations

### 4.1    Labour Department

This government department plays an important role in construction safety and health at work in terms of law enforcement and employees' compensation. (Information about the Labour Department is available at www.info.gov.hk/labour/.) In 2001, there are 28 divisions in the Labour Department, two of which are particularly related to construction safety and site accidents.

1.   Operations Division

The Operations Division (OD) aims to promote the safety and health of those working in industrial undertakings, including building and engineering construction sites. The OD carries out routine inspections to construction sites in order to advice site management staff to maintain and improve site safety standard.

2.   Legal Services Division

This division aims at enforcing the relevant legislation in Hong Kong. According to the Report of the Commissioner for Labour 2001, in that year there were 1,460 numbers of building and engineering construction summonses convicted under the Factories and Industrial Undertakings Ordinance and subsidiary legislation, with  total fines in the amount of HK$26,256,350. The average fine per convicted case was HK$17,984.

### 4.2    Occupational Safety and Health Council (OSHC)

Established in 1988, the objective of this statutory body is to promote occupational safety and health in Hong Kong. Functions organized by the OSHC include public lectures, safety and health campaigns, training courses, and the publication of an official OSHC monthly journal entitled Green Cross. The OSHC web site is: www.oshc.org.hk.

### 4.3    Safety Specialist Group of the Hong Kong Institution of Engineers

The Safety Specialist Group (SSG) was established within the Hong Kong Institution of Engineers since December 1995. The mission of the SSG is 'to promote safety awareness of engineers, and uphold and improve safety standards in engineering practice through the promotion, development and dissemination of information and knowledge'. The SSG web site is: www. hkiessg.com. The organization of SSG consists of a Committee, and its activities and functions are executed by four Task Teams:

1.  Task Team for Education and Training

2.  Task Team for Liaison and Publicity

3.  Task Team for Publication and Information

4.  Task Team for Technical and Social Activities

## 5.  Insurance, Compensation and Costs of Accidents

The Hong Kong employees' compensation system is a non-fault, non-contributory system funded by the payment of insurance premiums by contractors to private insurance companies. As required by the Employees' Compensation Ordinance (ECO), it is compulsory for contractors to insure against any compensations and common law claim for damages that they may be liable for because of work injury to their workers. Up to 2001, the maximum amount of compensation payable to injuries and deaths arising out of and in the course of work are HK$2,016,000 and HK$1,764,000 respectively. According to the ECO, an income ceiling of HK$21,000 is applicable for the purpose of compensation calculation.

In addition to receiving compensation as stipulated by the ECO, injured workers in Hong Kong are eligible to claim damages by common law in tort. Usually the amount of damages obtainable from legal proceedings is much higher than the compensation receivable from the ECO. However, it may take years before the completion of the formal legal process and the award of damages.

The contractor's possible losses in monetary terms due to accidents are listed below:

### 5.1  Direct Costs

1.  Medical treatment — The worker injured in an accident requires appropriate medical treatment. If the fee is not covered by an insurance scheme, then it is the contractor's obligation to pay for the expenses incurred out of his own pocket.

2.   Damage to equipment and finished work — Some parts of the equipment and finished work may be damaged in an accident. Again the contractor is liable to pay for the repair fees of the machines and the damaged work.

3.   Stoppage of work — Work is usually stopped after the occurrence of an accident. This is because the authority will have to examine, inspect and analyse the causes of accident on site. Workers always slow down their work or even stop working because of psychological effect and curiosity. It takes time to repair the damaged work and equipment before normal work is resumed. Sometimes work is delayed due to the absence of the injured worker. The replacement usually requires time to become familiar with the work.

4.   Compensation — In general, the expenses of the injured persons or damaged parts of work are well covered by insurance protection schemes. However, records have shown that in many cases the contractor pays an additional sum of money, to compensate the worker's physical injuries, as a moral obligation.

5.   Administration — After an accident a member of staff will be appointed to look after the entire event. Various documents are involved in connection with the accident, particularly a report on the causes of the accident and the possible measures to prevent similar occurrences.

6.   Fines — Fines may be imposed by the court and there are other associated expenses to be paid by the contractor as a result of legal actions taken by the authority or the injured person.

## 5.2    Indirect Costs

1.   Inefficiency — As mentioned previously, workers slow down naturally after the occurrence of serious accidents. Most people tend to re-think and re-consider their working procedures. The overall productivity rate of the whole construction team on site may be lowered.

2.   Loss of future contract — There is no direct implication that a contractor bearing a poor safety record will be disqualified for tendering. However, the competitiveness of a contractor is affected by the remarks of the engineer who always considers safety performance of the contractor. When contractors of similar background and experience are bidding for

the same contract, consideration will always be given to the one who holds a better safety record.

3. Increase in insurance premium — Determination of the insurance premium largely depends on the risk of the job and the past performance of the insured workers. A contractor with a high frequency of accidents is usually required to pay higher insurance fees.

## 6. Education and Training

'There are also continuous demands of safety education for professionals, such as site managers and engineers, as well as the safety toolbox training for site personnel. No doubt, safety education and training are the most effective methods to promote construction safety in the long run.' (Wong and Cheung 1996)

### 6.1 Construction Industry Training Authority (CITA)

CITA is the key institute for the training of construction workers, tradesmen, and operatives. It offers full-time and part-time training courses for both new entrants to the construction industry, who know little or nothing about construction, and workers who are already working in the construction industry but want to upgrade their knowledge in construction. The CITA web site is: cita.edu.hk.

CITA also conducts certification for plant operators. In order to reduce the number of accidents associated with lifting appliances and lifting gears, the Factories and Industrial Undertakings (Lifting Appliances and Lifting Gear) Regulations were revised in 1994, requiring plant operators of the following lifting operations to be properly trained and certified:

1. Crawler-mounted mobile crane operation
2. Truck-mounted crane operation
3. Tower crane operation
4. Wheeled telescopic mobile crane operation

## 6.2 Vocational Training Council (VTC)

VTC is responsible for the provision of vocational education and vocational training in Hong Kong. It provides safety education in the syllabuses of various courses to personnel from different industries including construction, clothing, hotel and engineering, etc. In essence, VTC's Hong Kong Institute of Vocational Education (IVE) is mainly responsible for the provision of vocational education, and VTC's training centres are responsible for the provision of vocational training. The VTC web site is: www.vtc.edu.hk.

## 6.3 Universities

Education and training for future construction professionals such as architects, engineers, builders and surveyors are mainly the responsibility of the universities. Safety training has become a very important element in the training at tertiary educational level. Universities also provide on-job-training safety courses for practitioners in the construction industry. The following courses are examples:

- Safety Auditors Training Scheme (SATS)
- Registered Safety Officer (RSO) Certificate
- Postgraduate Scheme in Occupational Safety & Health (POSH)
- Continuing Education Higher Certificate (CEHC) in Occupational Safety and Health. Graduates of CEHC who have three years experience in occupational safety and health may apply for full corporate membership (MIOSH) of the Institution of Occupational Safety and Health.

## 7. Safety Officer and Safety Supervisor

The Legislative Council in Hong Kong passed the Factories and Industrial Undertakings (Safety Officers and Safety Supervisors) Regulations in October 1986. In accordance with these regulations, the registration of safety officers started in December of the same year. The regulations also include the compulsory employment of safety officers and safety supervisors in the construction industry.

According to the regulations, which were revised in June 1995, a principal contractor or a specialist contractor employing 100 or more workers on a construction site or sites, is required to employ one registered safety officer on full time basis. In addition, one safety supervisor must be employed at each construction site, on which 20 or more workers are employed.

An advisory committee is in place to scrutinize the applications for the registration of safety officers. The committee consists of safety officers and representatives from the Labour Department, the construction industry, and institutions which provide training for industrial safety.

## 7.1 Duties of a Safety Officer

The principal duty of a safety officer is to assist the proprietor of the industrial undertaking in promoting the safety and health of his employees. The safety officer's specific duties include:

1. To advise the proprietor on measures to be taken in the interest of the safety and health of persons employed, and implement such measures once they are approved by the proprietor
2. To inspect the industrial undertakings and determine whether there is any machinery, plant, equipment, appliance or process which may be liable to cause bodily injury
3. To report the findings of the inspection to the proprietor and recommend suitable measures to be taken
4. To supervise safety supervisors
5. To advise the proprietor of any repairs or maintenance necessary in respect of the premises, plant, appliance, or equipment used
6. To investigate and report to the proprietor any accident, dangerous occurrences, injuries or fatal accidents, and make recommendations to prevent the happening of similar events
7. To receive, discuss, and countersign weekly reports submitted by safety supervisors
8. To prepare and submit a monthly safety report to the proprietor

## 7.2 Duties of a Safety Supervisor

The principal duties of a safety supervisor are to assist the safety officer in carrying out the latter's duties and to assist the proprietor of the industrial undertakings in promoting the safety and health of the employees. The safety supervisor's specific duties include:

1. To give suggestions to the proprietor or safety officer on safety precautions, which the employees have to take
2. To ensure that work is being carried out safely
3. To prepare and submit a weekly safety report to the proprietor.

## 8.   Conclusion

In the past, construction project management usually focused on three major items: time, cost and quality. Nowadays, construction project managers on site have to integrate five facets in their management practice. They are time, cost, quality, safety and environment, all of equal importance. Safety has become a major consideration for all site personnel, both from the industrial and the social points of view.

Significant contributions have to be made by five major parties in order to sustain a high level of safety performance for the local construction industry in the long run. The parties are the government, clients, consultants, contractors, and individual site staff.

The government, as the legislation and law enforcement body, must ensure that safety legislation is appropriate and up-to-date. The clients, who finance construction developments, should put a stronger emphasis on construction safety, by selecting contractors who are not only submitting lowest tenders, but have good safety track records. The consultants, including the architects, have to ensure that their designs are free from safety and health hazards to workers during construction and to end-users after project completion. The contractors, particularly the main contractors, must establish, implement, and develop a comprehensive safety system for their companies as well as for construction sites. Finally, the site staff must upkeep and upgrade their knowledge in construction safety by attending safety-training activities such as formal training courses, safety seminars, and toolbox talks. They have to be aware of safety hazards on site, and to fully understand their safety responsibilities, both moral and legal, for themselves, their co-workers, and other people in the neighbourhood of their construction sites.

# 9

# SITE ADMINISTRATION AND CONTROL

## 1. Introduction

A construction project consumes a large amount of resources, yet it has to be completed on time while satisfying the quality and budget requirements. In recent years, more stringent restrictions on safety and sustainability issues have also been imposed. During construction, proper administration and control of the works in various aspects is necessary so as to satisfy the above mentioned requirements. This chapter will cover the common aspects in site administration and control.

## 2. Client's Control

A client who has a need for a construction project usually appoints two specialists to achieve the goal: an engineer to design the works and a contractor to convert the design into the physical product.

Normally the client would not control directly the processes of the construction works. A professional engineer is required to design the works and supervise the construction. The client selects and appoints the engineer by experience or based on some sort of competition, such as the firm producing the best design or proposing the lowest fee for the design. The appointed engineer will carry out the duties and exercise the authority specified in or implied from the conditions of contract.

The amount of control the client wishes to exercise can be reflected in the type of construction contract adopted for the project. The client will bear different levels of risk by exercising different degrees of control on different types of contract. The client will have day-to-day control of a cost plus contract but relatively little control on a lump sum contract. For a design and build contract, the client will bear a relatively low risk.

## 3.    Engineer's Control

In the conventional contract of design by engineer and construction by contractor, the client's control is delegated to the engineer, and in turn to the engineer's representative (ER). The ERs should act impartially in carrying out their duties, though they are paid by the client and sometimes they may be direct employees of the client.

The ER's main duty is to check and confirm that the contractor has carried out the duties as specified in the contract. These include the use of proper materials, the right level of workmanship, and progress in accordance with the contract requirements. The actual extent of the duty will depend on the type of contract and the delegation by the engineer or approval by the client. In general, the ER's duties are:

1.  Administration: To organize site staff and assign appropriate duties in supervising the construction works.

2.  Works: To supervise the construction of the works to the requirements of the contract, including checking and testing of the raw materials, the preformed components and the final product.

3.  Payment: To certify payment to the contractor on the amount of work satisfactorily completed.

4.  Records: To keep records of all kinds on site and to produce the evidence whenever it is required.

## 4.    Subcontracting

The contractor would not be allowed to subcontract the whole of the works. The contractor should be permitted to subcontract parts of the works on certain terms as specified in the contract.

One basic requirement is that prior to subcontracting any part of the works, the contractor should submit all necessary information to the engineer for approval. The information should include the full particulars of the works to be subcontracted, the particulars of the proposed subcontractor and the subcontract terms and conditions.

If necessary, the engineer has full power to order the removal of any sub-contractor from the site, despite previously giving consent to subcontract.

## 5.    Site Progress Monitoring

One of the duties of the ER is to monitor the progress of the construction work undertaken by the contractor. From time to time, the actual progress is compared with the planned one. A progress chart is used to record the actual progress of each activity of a project. Very often the programme and the progress chart are combined into one so that comparison can conveniently be made.

There are many forms of the combined programme and progress charts. The exact form to be adopted is determined by the contents and nature of the contract.

### 5.1    Bar Chart

The simplest form for recording the progress on a programme chart is based on a bar chart. The key activities are shown by bars of certain lengths representing the time and the total amount of work to be completed. The percentages at various stages indicate the cumulative quantity of work to be done with respect to the time of the project. The line drawn below each bar indicates the actual date of commencement for the particular item of work, with the cumulative percentages of work completed with respect to the estimated work to date, and also the date of completion, if applicable.

This chart shows the following information that can be used in monitoring the progress:

- Date of commencement and completion of an item of work relative to the proposed dates
- The time duration in advance of or behind the schedule for the activity concerned
- The proportion of the item completed to date, compared with the estimated amount of work, and the amount of work to be done

## 5.2    Pictorial Progress Chart

In many instances, the progress of works is best presented in a diagram. Jobs such as laying of a pipeline, site formation with cutting and filling, tunnel construction, highway construction and erection of a multi-storey building etc. are best illustrated using the pictorial progress charts. The progress with respect to the programme is shown on the same diagram, thus enabling easy comparison.

## 5.3    Financial Progress Chart

The payment records compared with the estimated payments can be shown by the financial progress chart, which consists of a number of curves including the following:

- The estimated and the actual expenditure curves
- The estimated and the actual income curves

To the contractor, the expenditure curve is a continuous curve whereas the income curve would be in step forms when monthly interim payment is adopted.

The financial progress chart can provide the following information:

- Comparison between the estimated and the actual accumulated expenditure as well as the revenue
- The percentage of work completed in money terms with respect to the contract sum
- The unexpected significant difference between the income and the expenditure

The information derived from this chart must be read in junction with the actual progress of the works, so as to draw meaningful conclusion on the progress of the project.

## 6. Records

As mentioned previously, one of the main duties of the ER is to keep adequate records. The reasons for maintaining the records are to:

- Enable an appraisal to be made on the progress of the work
- Form the basis for fixing fair rewards to the contractor
- Enable all materials to be ordered in good time
- Assure designers that the design assumptions are valid
- Form a source of information to solve new problems that may arise during construction
- Explain the subsequent behaviour of the completed works
- Form the evidence as records of facts in times of dispute
- Keep the information as required under the law

### 6.1 Appraisal on the Progress of the Work

Under the contract, the contractor is required to produce a programme for the execution of the works. When the actual progress of work on site is compared with the programme, activities which fall behind or in advance of the schedule can be identified. In the former case, remedial measures may be necessary so as not to affect the critical activities and subsequently extend the project duration.

### 6.2 Fixing Rewards to the Contractor

In most construction projects, the contractor receives interim payments based on the amount of work completed satisfactorily. Throughout the contract duration, the agreed amount of work completed and the rate of completion must therefore be recorded accurately. These records of work completion are submitted to the engineer for the purpose of certifying the interim payments. Timely payments by the client will help the contractor in financial planning.

### 6.3 Ordering Materials in Good Time

Since construction activities consume a variety of materials in large quantities, sufficient stock of materials is crucial to prevent delay due to shortage or late delivery of materials. It is always only possible to stack limited amount of materials on site. In Hong Kong, the rate of consumption, the transportation facilities and the limited storage space on site have to be taken into consideration in planning the stock level. Therefore, it is important to check records of the available stock on site periodically or whenever the need arises, and compare them with the amounts estimated to be required so that appropriate quantities of materials will be ordered in good time. Delays in the programme due to a shortage of materials must be avoided.

## 6.4  Validating Design Assumptions

During the design process, assumptions have to be made for certain factors or parameters of a construction project no matter how intensive or how detailed the site has been investigated. This is particularly true when considering subsurface conditions such as the seasonal variation of groundwater level. In operations where excavation is required — such as foundation works, laying of underground pipeline and basement construction — the soil will be exposed. Records of soil conditions, therefore, could provide very useful information for verifying the assumptions made in design. If there is a substantial deviation from the assumptions, modifications or alteration of the design will become necessary.

## 6.5  Solving New Problems

The contractor faces numerous operational problems and difficulties throughout the construction period. The contractor may have a new problem by trial and error based on experience, or eventually seek advice from the experts or specialists concerned. In any case, records of previous construction work, whether on the same site or not, will be valuable in solving similar problems that may arise in the future.

## 6.6  Explaining Subsequent Behaviour

The physical completion of a construction project does not imply an end to every party involved in the project. Sometimes it may be necessary to reveal the history of certain construction activity particularly in times of disputes. For example, if construction defects are found, the previous quality records of materials used, the details of the construction process, the test results of the components and the final product, and perhaps the weather conditions at the time of construction may help explain the situation. Another example is that in deciding the type of foundations for a redevelopment area, records of existing foundations and their performance will be useful. The compiling of all relevant information at the construction stage forms a set of useful documents for future reference.

## 6.7    Recording Facts or Evidence

True records of what have happened on site or work done or not done by parties can be important and useful in determining the causes of failures or accidents on site. These documents are particular useful in legal proceedings. Likewise, a record of the design calculation of temporary works and their actual erection would serve as reliable evidence in investigating the accidents or failures during construction.

## 6.8    Complying With Requirements Under the Law

In accordance with the Factories and Industrial Undertakings (Safety Officers and Safety Supervisors) Regulations, reports submitted by the safety officers and supervisors must be kept for a period of three years after the date of discussion between the contractor and the safety officer. Other certificates, such as testing of the lifting equipment or mechanical plant, are also kept for similar purposes.

## 7.    Types of Records

Broadly speaking, records of construction activities can be classified into four main categories:

- Historical records
- Quantitative and financial records
- Qualitative records
- 'As constructed' records

## 7.1    Historical records

Historical records show the history, i.e. the progress of implementing the works stage by stage. All relevant information regarding the construction on site, such as the weather condition, the type of soil encountered during excavation, the actual progress and so on will be included. The common historical records include Inspector's Daily Return, Site Diary, Weekly and Monthly Reports and Site Instructions are detailed below.

### 7.1.1    Inspector's Daily Return

One of the duties of the inspector is to visit all areas of the site at least once a day. In his visit he records:

- The type and extent of work being carried out during the day
- The number of labourers working in each part of the project
- The type and the number of plant employed, including those that are idling
- Any delay of activities on site
- Any particular event happened on site

The Inspector's Daily Return should include detailed information on the above-mentioned items. It provides a complete picture of what have happened on site. Upon receipt of a copy of the return, staff in the design office is able to understand and appreciate the current activities taking place and the progress made on site. Whenever there is any dispute with the contractor, such as the progress or payment for extra works, reference can then be made to these records.

### 7.1.2 Site Diary

The Site Diary is a formal record of the progress of the works including any events which may have affected the progress and quality of the finished works. This document usually includes:

- The date and weather conditions
- The number of workers in various trades
- Materials delivered to the site, the quantity used and retained
- Items of plant on site, working or idling, including reasons for being idle
- Any concreting activity, the location and quantity of the mixes poured
- A brief description of the completed work with the approximate amount done
- Any work carried out in connection with the utility service
- Instructions issued to the contractor

Having checked and agreed on all information which is entered by the site foreman or the inspector, the site agent who is the contractor's representative, will sign the Site Diary.

### 7.1.3 Engineer's Representative's Diary

While the records discussed so far are mostly related to the construction works, the Engineer Representative's diary can be a personal and confidential document. The ER records his observation of the works and all decisions made including any instructions given during the day, particularly when disputes have arisen. Sometimes the ER writes down particular points about the works or performance of site staff, which he does not wish to disclose at that time but would like to discuss with his staff or the site agent later.

### 7.1.4 Weekly Report and Monthly Report

The Weekly Report summarizes the progress of work in a particular week and includes other relevant information such as problems which have caused delays, together with the course of action being taken to overcome them. This is a report sent regularly to the engineer by the ER.

The contents of the Monthly Report is similar to those of the Weekly Report. It gives a more general summary of progress in the month and includes expenditure figures. This report should be presented in a form suitable for perusal by the client as well. Normally the ER prepares the draft. The engineer will revise if necessary and send it to the client. Occasionally, for overseas jobs, the ER acts on behalf of the engineer and submits the report direct to the client.

### 7.1.5 Site Instructions

It is very often necessary to confirm or change the details of the works, though they are generally of minor issue. The information may include setting out data, shuttering fixing details, materials to be ordered, remedial works proposals and reminders. A simple system of issuing notes to the contractor is thus necessary. The staff in the ER's office usually prepares their notes on a standard book. This is called a book of Site Instructions. The notes can be typed or handwritten, with necessary sketches for illustrative purpose and signed by the person who has prepared the instruction. Both the original and the duplicate are handed to the site agent who keeps the original and acknowledges receipt on the duplicate which remains in the book. The duplicate copy is then sent back to the ER's office for record. The duplicate copies remaining in the book represent a log of instructions sent to the site agent. By inspecting the book the ER knows what instructions his staff members have been giving to the contractor. Many small but can be important matters are dealt with using this system. Sometimes verbal instructions are given on the spot and are confirmed later by issuing the site instruction.

### 7.1.6 Progress Photographs and Video Recording

Sometimes visual and even sound records are required by taking progress photographs or recording videos.

The main reasons for keeping these kinds of record are:

- To keep a permanent visual and sometimes audio record of the progress of the works
- To show a particular feature of the work which will generally be covered up later
- For publicity purposes

These records are dated and are fully labelled with the location and purpose of recording. In cases where the scale effect is not apparent, a suitable recognizable item is included for better comparison. Photographs and videos are usually taken at regular intervals from the same location, though this may not always be possible because of the nature and the pace of construction.

### 7.1.7    Site Meeting Minutes

Site meetings, chaired by the engineer or ER, are held once a month. The meeting is attended by the engineer's supervisory staff, the contractor's representatives and sub-contractors. Problems encountered, the work programme and progress recorded, actions to be taken etc., together with any other relevant matters will be discussed and resolved at the meeting. After the meeting, a copy of the minutes is sent to the contractor for his confirmation, retention as well as action if necessary.

## 7.2    Quantitative and Financial Records

The ER prepares the quantitative and financial records for payment to the contractor.  These record the measurements of all kinds of works that have been completed and form a basis for payment to the contractor. The common documents in connection with the payment are site measurement books, interim statements, orders for extra works and daywork accounts.

The ER will also prepare the monthly financial report to the client, providing information in regard to expenditure forecast and estimated final contract sum. Summary of claims and potential charges will draw the client's attention to any potential expenditure. Estimates for any potential variations will enable the client to make decisions for design or variation options.

### 7.2.1    Site Measurement Book

In the preparation of tender documents, the quantity of each item of work is first taken from tender drawings, entered on a taking off sheet, summarized on an abstract sheet and then entered into the bill of quantities. On site, the procedure for measuring the portion of completed works can be similar. All measurements are entered in the site measurement book. The quantities measured are gathered on abstract sheets before they are compiled into a statement of the total value of the finished portion of work.

Methods of measurement can vary for different jobs. Nevertheless the record should show clearly what has been measured and agreed between the ER and the site agent, and what has not. In addition, quantities that have been paid for should be distinguished from what has been measured.

To aid the verification of the calculation, the records should incorporate:

- Sketches and dimensions of work as executed, which are prepared for the sake of easy understanding and checking
- The detailed working of the quantities
- A summary of the quantities worked out, preferably classified in the same order as that in the bill of quantities
- A summary of quantities agreed for payment on each certificate

It is essential that all measurement data, figures and calculations are accurate, clear and sufficient, as these records form the basis for determining the payment to the contractor.

## 7.2.2  Interim Statements (The Government of Hong Kong SAR 1999)

Usually the contractual arrangement is restricted to the re-measurement contract with drawings, specifications and bills of quantities and the contractor is paid at monthly intervals according to the value of the portion of the works finished satisfactorily. Every month the contractor submits to the engineer, via the ER, a statement of the work completed in that month. Within 21 days (or as specified in the contract) of submission, the engineer will value and certify the statement and the client will pay the amount within the next 21 days (or otherwise specified in the contract). If the client fails to pay the contractor within the time agreed, the contractor is entitled to ask for interest as well as the overdue payment.

The interim payment is based on:

- The estimated value of the permanent work executed
- The estimated value of temporary works or preliminary items as provided in the contract
- The estimated value of materials stored on site for permanent works construction

- The estimated sums payable to nominated subcontractors
- Any other sums the contractor is entitled to under the contract, e.g. the fluctuation clause

The sum is adjusted for:

- Previous payments on the works completed with satisfaction
- The limit of the retention money or the retention of a percentage of the total contract sum as required in the contract
- The cost of materials supplied by the client
- Liquidated damages
- The fluctuation in the cost of labour, material and plant

It is common for a contract to specify that a certain percentage of the payment for the total value of the work is retained by the client during construction. This is called retention money. Half of the money will usually be paid back to the contractor when the completion certificate is issued and the balance will be released at the end of the maintenance period. Sometimes the whole amount of the retention money is only released after the issue of maintenance certificate by the engineer.

The liquidated damage is the estimated damage or loss that the client will suffer if the works are not completed on time. It may include the client's loss in revenue from the works completed, the interest on capital investment and any extra cost for site supervision.

Very often there is a minimum value for each interim payment. The amount can be taken as 60% to 80% of the estimated contract sum divided by the number of months required for the completion of the works. For larger contracts the amount to be paid each month may be specified.

By the time the works are substantially completed with satisfaction, the engineer will issue a completion certificate to the contractor to indicate that he is satisfied with the completion of the work so far. The maintenance period then begins.

At the end of the maintenance period the work must be delivered to the client in as good a condition as it was at the beginning of the period. During this period any defect must be made good and any outstanding work must be completed. Otherwise the client is entitled to withhold the balance of the retention money and ask any other party to complete the outstanding work at the contractor's expense. If the work has been completed and maintained satisfactorily, the engineer will issue a maintenance certificate to the contractor.

### 7.2.3 Final Payment (The Government of Hong Kong SAR 1999)

Bills of quantities are commonly prepared by consultants for contractor to price. All items will be re-measured in the preparation of the final accounts. Any errors in the quantities will be rectified in the final re-measurement. Within three months (or a period specified in the contract) after the issue of the maintenance certificate for the construction work, the contractor submits a statement of the final account to the engineer. This will include a detailed assessment of the value of the work done and other sums which the contractor considers he is entitled to. Within another three months (or specified otherwise) of receipt of the final account or within three months (or as specified) from the expiry of the maintenance period, whichever is longer, the engineer will issue a final payment certificate confirming the total value of the project and the balance payable to the contractor. Such a sum should be paid within a specified period (e.g. 28 days) from the issuing date of the certificate.

The final account contains the following items:

- Preliminaries in the original bill of quantities plus approved adjustments and variations
- Remeasurement of the completed works
- Daywork accounts
- Adjustment due to price fluctuations in labour, materials and plant
- Payment for justified claims
- Supplemental agreements for some large infrastructure projects
- Deduction of materials supplied by the client
- Release of retention money
- Bonus payment or deduction for liquidated damages, if any

### 7.2.4 Variation Order and Daywork

Under a civil engineering contract the engineer has the authority to change any part of the works he thinks necessary for the completion of the works. The variation may include changes to any sequence, method or timing of construction specified in the contract that are desirable to achieve satisfactory or timely completion, improved or more economic functioning, or even for aesthetic reasons.

In many cases, varied works instructed are not of a character similar or executed under the same or similar conditions. In these cases, a rate has to be agreed between the engineer and the contractor. If both parties fail to reach an agreement, the engineer will fix a reasonable rate. On some occasions, the engineer may authorize the contractor to carry out extra work on a daywork basis. Daywork means the valuation of work according to the time spent by the workmen, the materials used and the plant employed plus an allowance on the profit and oncosts on the varied work.

Payment for dayworks is made as follows:

- Labour — labour rates for dayworks are priced by contractors in the tender. The percentage adjustment to these labour rates are also inserted in the tender for different working hours such as working overtime and working at night time. The priced labour rates should have contained profit and overhead.

- Plant — plant rates usually based on 'Hong Kong Construction Association (HKCA) Schedules for Plant Used in Dayworks Carried Out Incidental to Contract Work' published by the HKCA. A percentage adjustment to the plant rates in the HKCA Schedule will also be inserted by contractors in the tender to suit different contractor's plant arrangements and includes contractor's profit and overhead.

- Materials — There is no material schedule for dayworks. An item in the bills of quantities will be provided for contractors to insert a percentage for adjusting all materials deployed for dayworks. The percentage should cover the contractor's overhead and profit. Material invoices should be submitted for payment purpose.

Usually the Inspector of Works or Works Supervisor will be delegated the authority to record and agree jointly with the contractor the resources deployed for dayworks, although the ER may countersign (still depend on delegation) the records.

### 7.2.5    Milestone Payment (Hong Kong Government 1992)

This is an alternative payment method apart from the conventional re-measurement method. The contractual arrangement is usually based on a lump sum contract or a mixture of lump sum and re-measurement contract that comprises drawings, specifications and pricing document. Milestone means the completion of a part of the works or the occurrence of an event identified as such in the schedule of milestones. Milestone certificate means the certificate to be issued by the engineer in relation to the achievement of milestones.

The pricing document includes the Schedule of Prices, the Schedule of Milestones and the Interim Payment Schedules. The works of a particular contract are divided into a number of Cost Centres, each of which, with the exception of the First Cost Centre (the Preliminaries and General Requirements) represents a major item or series of interrelated items associated with the works. Cost Centres are named according to their general scope of works. The Schedule of Prices describes the items included in each Cost Centre and shows prices entered against all items contained in each Cost Centre.

The Schedule of Milestones identifies as milestones certain essential or significant steps towards the completion of the work within each Cost Centre, together with periods in months within which a contractor must achieve each milestone in order to maintain interim payments in accordance with the contract.

At the beginning of each calendar month, the engineer will issue to the contractor a Milestone Certificate stating whether on not any milestones should have been achieved during the preceding month. The Milestone Certificate then determines the Interim Payment Schedule percentage to be applied against each Cost Centre for the preparation of interim payment for the period corresponding to the Milestone Certificate.

The interim payment schedules set out the maximum accumulative percentage of each Cost Centre value in relation to each month for which the contractor may apply for payment, subject to the achievement of milestones and to application for payment as follows.

At the beginning of each month the contractor may apply to the engineer for an interim payment in relating to the preceding month. Each application should state:

- The amount claimed to be payable setting out the percentage of each cost center value claimed according to the Interim Payment Schedule
- Any other amount claimed to be payable, including sums payable to approved subcontractors

Each application should be accompanied by the monthly progress report and the Milestone Certificate for the month to which the application for interim payment relates.

The engineer should issue to the client, with a copy to the contractor, an interim payment certificate showing the amount payable to the contractor by way of interim payment within 28 days (or otherwise specified) following the date upon which the contractor submitted an application for interim payment. Such interim payment should include:

1. The amounts shown to be due by reference to the Interim Payment Schedules.
2. The amounts determined by the engineer to be paid in respect of:
   - The cost incurred
   - The works executed on a daywork basis
   - Any other allowance to which the contractor is entitled under the contract less:
     (i) The retention money
     (ii) Any amounts paid previously
     (iii) Any amounts recoverable from the contractor in accordance with the contract

In the event of the contractor's failure to achieve any milestone, the engineer will follow the procedures below for certifying payments:

(a) All payments relating to the Cost Centre in which the milestone in questions has not been achieved should be suspended at the amount determined by reference to the percentage appearing in the Interim Payment Schedules applicable to the month in which the milestone was due to have been achieved.

(b) Payments suspended in (a) above should be resumed by being included in the next application for interim payment made after the milestone is achieved at the amount determined by reference to the percentage appearing in the Interim Payment Schedules applicable to the month in which the milestone was due to have been achieved.

(c) The Interim Payment Schedules should be revised by the engineer within 21 days (or a specified period) of receipt of an application for resumption of payments in (b) above to take account of:

- The date by which the milestone next following the non-achieved milestone is likely to be achieved

- Any subsequent milestone which is not likely to be achieved by its stipulated date
- The earliest subsequent milestone which is likely to be achieved by its stipulated date

## 7.3 Qualitative Records

All materials used in the construction works should be of the quality required under the contract and are subject to testing. The contractor is obliged to provide all assistance and necessary equipment for carrying out the tests on site and, if possible, at the place of manufacture.

These test records are important in certifying that the materials are in compliance with the contract specifications and in assessing their performance. If any records are lost, the engineer will be in the dark, and further tests on the finished works will cause delays and can be expensive and time consuming.

The following are some of the common tests conducted in civil engineering works:

- Borehole records
- Grading analysis of fill materials and aggregates
- Proctor density tests
- In-situ density tests
- Concrete cube tests
- Test of reinforcing bars
- Watertightness tests for pipes and water retaining structures

In addition, the contractor is required to establish a quality assurance system for the control of all design and construction activities so as to facilitate completion of the works. At the start of the contract the contractor needs to submit a proposed quality plan to the engineer for approval. The contractor also appoints a suitable qualified and experienced person as manager of the quality assurance system to ensure effective operation of the system.

## 7.4 'As Constructed' Records

The 'as constructed' records contain all the details of the actual works completed. Basically information for the record drawings is obtained from working drawings and modified according to site instructions, variation orders and, above all, records of the actual construction.

Keeping 'as constructed' records is very important. Many site staff may have come across situations where records of previously built structures are missing. A lot of unnecessary work has to be done, while costing extra money and requiring more time, to locate, say, the underground drains for a particular project.

The information recorded on the drawings should be as detailed as possible. Taking the example of the laying of a pipeline, the following information should be included:

- The exact alignment of pipeline
- Pipe material
- Pipe diameter
- Pipe joints
- Invert level
- Type of bedding
- Location of joints, bends, tapers, valves, manholes
- Results of watertightness testing

The ER should ensure that 'as constructed' records are made continuously throughout the construction period. If this is not done, at the end of the contract the ER will be facing such a large pile of drawings and sketches that it is often difficult to retrieve the relevant information to prepare the record drawings.

## 7.5   The Contractor's Records

The records discussed so far are mostly records kept by the resident engineer. The contractor will maintain similar records for comparison and record purposes. In accordance with the contract requirements, the contractor should keep the completed, up to date records of all transactions entered into by the contractor including copies of subcontracts, purchase orders, correspondence, manufacturer's specification, minutes of meetings and documents relating to procurement of equipment and materials, personal matter such as salary records and financial claims.

## 8.   Delays

During the contract period, construction work may have to be stopped for a variety of reasons. This can cause progress to fall behind the original schedule. The site staff should be aware of the common reasons and always plan ahead to prevent their occurrence, and minimize their impact in case they happen.

The common reasons for causing delays are:

- Design changes
- Rework
- Inclement weather
- Shortage of materials
- Breakdown of plant or equipment
- Workforce strikes
- Accidents

## 8.1 Design Changes

Changes in design are very common during construction. The reasons for the changes are insufficient site investigation, change of mind of the client as a result of variation of market demands and inexperienced design input. The contractor has to wait for the revised information or move to other parts of work. If this is concerned with the critical activities, it will result in the delay of the whole construction project.

## 8.2 Rework

When the construction work is not up to standard or if defects are identified, the engineer will demand remedial measures or rework by the contractor. In the worst cases, some of the completed works would have to be demolished. This would certainly lead to a lot of extra work and effort, and delays.

## 8.3 Inclement Weather

The pace of construction work is often affected by adverse weather conditions. Most civil engineering construction projects such as foundation and site formation works are done in the open, and are affected by inclement weather. For safety reasons, these kinds of works must be stopped in heavy rain or strong wind.

The delay of the works due to bad weather may allow the contractor to claim for extension of time for the project, but this must be justified by what have been recorded in the weather charts or confirmed with the Hong Kong Observatory. The delay in one small section of the project may lead to the delay in completing the whole project, which is against the interest of the client. If no extension of time is allowed in the contract, the contractor must make allowance for this kind of delay during initial planning and make up the delay by whatever means.

As the delay has such an important impact on the completion date, the actual weather conditions must be properly recorded. Inclement weather causes not only stoppages but also damages to the construction works. The result is that the contractor has to rectify the damages at his own costs.

## 8.4 Shortage of Materials

As required in the contract, the contractor provides all labour, materials and plant in the execution of the works. To achieve the progress as proposed in the programme, the contractor should maintain all necessary resources in sufficient quantities. There is no allowance for extension of time due to shortage of materials.

Construction work requires a large variety of materials and in considerable quantities. Some materials are available locally but many have to be imported from other countries. Due attention must be paid to the planning of the delivery of materials when a lot of materials is ordered. The engineer will check the orders placed by the contractor to avoid any stoppage of work due to shortage of materials.

## 8.5 Breakdown of Plant

Plant is another important resource in modern construction. The use of plant to replace manual labour normally reduces the completion time of the project. If the plant breaks down or does not work properly, it should be repaired or replaced, otherwise progress will be affected. There is also no allowance for extension of time due to breakdown of plant.

## 8.6 Strikes

Construction works can be stopped if there are strikes. In Hong Kong failure of the subcontractor to pay the agreed wages to workers sometimes leads to strikes. The engineer should record the exact duration of a strike, the damage that may have been caused to the works, and any safety precautions not properly observed during the period. The engineer will assess the extent of damage to the project while the contractor will be required to make up the possible delay of work. Such a delay is not justified for consideration of extension of time.

## 8.7  Accidents

The Hong Kong construction industry has a very high accident rate. The causes of accidents are numerous, for example, safety measures have not been properly observed — workers do not wear the personal protection equipment provided, such as the safety helmet. In the other cases accident may occur if the temporary access is not sufficiently secure.

In case of an accident or if a worker is injured, the contractor has to notify the Commissioner for Labour and forward a report on the incident to the engineer. There may be delay to the works since the area concerned has to be closed for investigation by the authorities. Extra work and time are required to clear the debris caused by the incident, to repair the damages, and to install additional safety and security measures. Psychologically the workers on site may have been affected by an accident and slow down their pace of work or even stop working altogether.

## Acknowledgement

*Mr H.M. Cheung's valuable suggestions for this chapter are gratefully acknowledged.*

# PART II

# QUANTITATIVE PROJECT MANAGEMENT

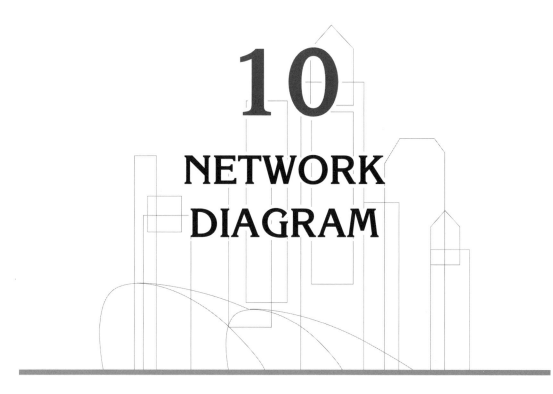

# 10

# NETWORK DIAGRAM

## 1. Introduction

A civil engineering project usually involves the implementation of a large number of interrelated activities. Careful planning and coordination is needed so that the activities can be carried out smoothly using minimum resources.

The arrangement of all the activities of a project in an appropriate sequence or set of sequences is called the **programming of works**. This is a very important job in all kinds of construction projects. In this and the next few chapters a systematic method of programming will be introduced.

## 2. The Traditional Method

In the traditional method of programming, the project planner (usually the contractor) presents **a programme chart** (also called a **bar chart** or **Gantt chart**). The activities involved in a project and the time taken for each activity is displayed in this chart.

Fig. 10.1 gives a typical example of such a programme.

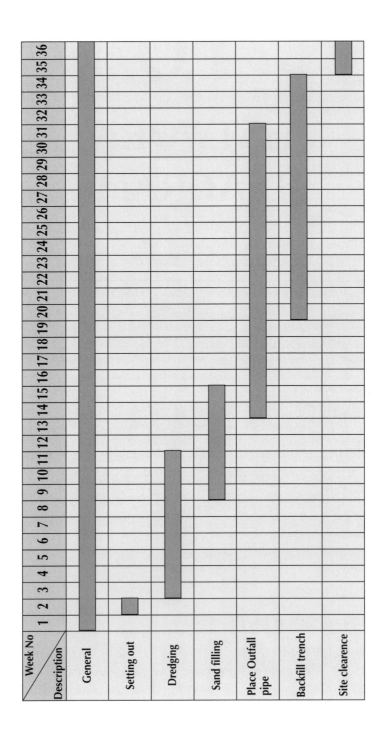

**Fig. 10.1**   An example of a programme chart.

In the past, the production of a programme chart depends very much on the intuition and experience of the planner. The traditional method of programming is not based on any theory. However, there are a couple of drawbacks that arise in this kind of approach.

Firstly a lot of details are missing in the chart. It does not indicate which critical activities must be finished on time so that the overall project will not be delayed. It therefore cannot help the planner to analyse the activities or make decisions about them.

The creation of such a traditional programme chart depends solely on the intuition and experience of the individual planner. The number of activities considered is therefore limited. Also, there is no objective, analytical or logical basis to produce the chart.

## 3. Network Diagrams

An improved method over the traditional method for the production of a work programme is the **critical path method**. This was introduced around 1957 to assist project planners to programme their work with the optimal use of resources.

Before the activities are analysed and the optimal resources found for a project, the project itself is first represented in a network diagram. In this chapter, we will see how such a network diagram can be drawn for a project. In the next chapter, you will see how the network diagram is analysed using the critical path method.

## 3.1 Producing an Activity List

To draw a network diagram for a project, the first step is to produce an **activity list** for the project. Table 10.1 gives an example of an activity list. This step is merely a brainstorming exercise. The activities thought of are not necessary listed in a logical order.

| Activity | Description |
|---|---|
| A | Bulk excavation |
| B | Excavation to column foundation |
| C | Binding layer |
| D | Concreting of foundation |
| . | . |
| . | . |
| . | . |
| . | . |
| . | . |

**Table 10.1** An activity list for a project. The number of activities can be up to a few hundreds in a big project. The activities listed are not necessary arranged in proper order.

### 3.2 Drawing the Network Diagram

The next step is to arrange the activities in a logical order and represent them in a network diagram.

The following conventions are usually used when we draw a network diagram for a project. The kind of network we are drawing are called activity-on-arrow (AOA) networks.

An activity in a project is represented by an arrow with two small circles (called **nodes**), one at its head and the other at its tail (Fig. 10.2).

**Fig. 10.2** An activity, labelled A, in an activity-on-arrow network.

Usually, numbers are put inside the nodes. Any number can be used to name a node as long as the number at the arrow head (i.e. end node) is greater than that at the tail (i.e. start node) of the activity. Fig. 10.2 shows a correct number entry while Fig. 10.3 shows an incorrect entry.

**Fig. 10.3** An INCORRECT number entry for the nodes of a certain activity A.

So in general an activity is denoted by two numbers, i-j, where j is greater than i. The numbers i and j may or may not be consecutive numbers.

Activity A in Fig. 10.2 can also be called activity 1-2.

If there are two activities, activity A and activity B, and activity B can commence only when activity A is completed, then they may be represented as shown in Fig. 10.4.

**Fig. 10.4** Network representing activity A followed by activity B.

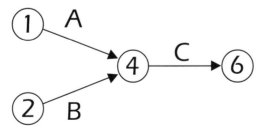

**Fig. 10.5** Another example of a network.

Let us now consider Fig. 10.5. The network tells us that activity A (or activity 1-4) and activity B (or activity 2-4) must be completed before activity C (or activity 4-6) can commence. Activities 1-4 and 2-4, however, can be carried out simultaneously.

### 3.3 Dummy Activities

The following example illustrates one use of a **dummy activity**. It is required to draw a network for a project which consists of activities A, B, C and D, such that A must be completed before C, and both A and B must be completed before D can commence.

The relationship between A, B and D can be represented as shown in Fig. 10. 6. However, activity C is difficult to be added to the diagram — C cannot start from node 5 since the completion of B is not a necessary requirement. Then, how can we add activity C to the diagram?

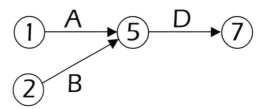

**Fig. 10.6**   Network representing A, B and D, but how about C?

The method is to invent an activity 5-6, a dummy activity, with no time duration and no cost incurred, so that activity C can start from node 5 and at the same time activity D can be drawn in to satisfy the requirements (Fig. 10.7).

Note that the dummy activity is drawn in as a dotted line.

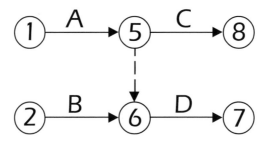

**Fig. 10.7**   Network for the problem showing the dummy activity 5-6.

The dummy activity does not take any time to complete, nor does it use any resources - it is used only to show the logic (or sequence) of the network.

Consider another situation in which a dummy activity is used. In Fig. 10.8, activity A is denoted by 1-3 and activity D is denoted by 5-7. Activities B and C, however, are both denoted by 3-5, which is not allowed in the network diagram convention. To rectify this situation, dummy activity 4-5 is introduced in the network so that the logical sequence is retained while at the same time each activity is represented by two unique nodes (Fig. 10.9).

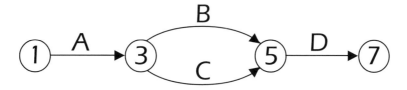

**Fig. 10.8**   An incorrect network diagram for activities A, B, C and D.

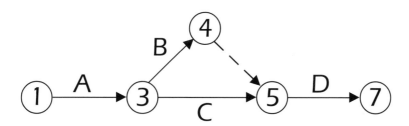

**Fig. 10.9**   A correct network representing activities A, B, C and D after dummy activity 4-5 has been introduced.

In this revised network, activities A, B, C and D are denoted by 1-3, 3-4, 3-5 and 5-7 respectively. Each activity therefore is uniquely denoted by two numbers.

## 4.   Examples

### 4.1   Example 1

A group of workers is preparing to erect two pylons. The activities involved are:

A   Obtain material
B   Obtain concrete mixer
C   Dig hole 1
D   Dig hole 2
E   Mix concrete
F   Set up pylon 1
G   Set up pylon 2
H   Pour concrete into hole 1
I   Pour concrete into hole 2

Pouring concrete into a particular hole must be done after the concrete is mixed and the corresponding pylon is set up. But before mixing the concrete, the workers have to obtain the material and the concrete mixer. Also a hole must be dug before the corresponding pylon can be set up. Because of limited labourers, only one hole can be dug at a time. Draw the network diagram for this project.

### Solution

We first draw the complete activity list (Table 10.2).

| Symbol | Activity description |
|--------|---------------------|
| A | Obtain material |
| B | Obtain concrete mixer |
| C | Dig hole 1 |
| D | Dig hole 2 |
| E | Mix concrete |
| F | Set up pylon 1 |
| G | Set up pylon 2 |
| H | Pour concrete into hole 1 |
| I | Pour concrete into hole 2 |

**Table 10.2**   The activity list.

To draw the network, start with activities which do not have to follow any other activities. They are A, B and C (Fig. 10.10).

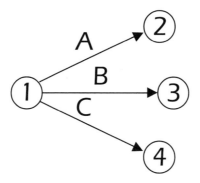

**Fig. 10.10** First part of the network.

Then the other activities are drawn into the network diagram as shown in Fig. 10.11.

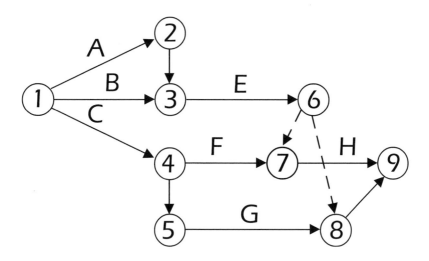

**Fig. 10.11** The complete network.

## 4.2    Example 2

Draw the network represented by the activities in Table 10.3. The project begins with Activities A and B and ends with K.

| Activities | Precedes |
|:---:|:---:|
| A | C |
| B | C,D |
| C | E,F |
| D | I,G,H |
| E | I |
| F | I |
| G | J |
| H | J |
| I | K |
| J | K |
| K | - |

**Table 10.3**    The second column gives activities which follow those in the first column.

## Solution

Notice that the activity list is different from what we have had. However, the network diagram is drawn in a similar way (Fig. 10.12).

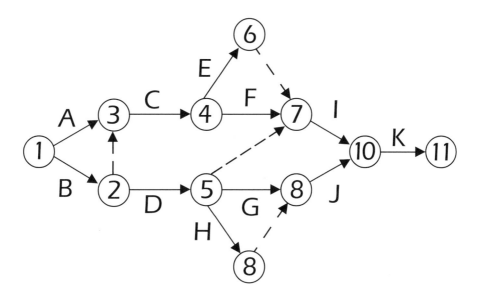

**Fig. 10.12** The final network diagram.

Note that the examples in this chapter are for illustration purpose only. They are therefore oversimplified when compared to actual situations in construction projects. In reality, tens or sometimes hundreds of activities are involved in a project and the networks developed are much greater in size and complexity. With these larger networks, computer programs have been developed to draw and subsequently analyse them.

The analysis of network diagrams will be discussed in the next chapter.

# 11

# CRITICAL
# PATH METHOD

## 1. Introduction

The representation of activities in a civil engineering project by a network diagram was discussed in the previous chapter. In this chapter, we are going to see that every project with activities that are to be programmed has at least one sequence of activities which is critical to the completion of that project. Any of the activities on this critical path which are not completed in the estimated period of duration will cause the overall project length to be extended. The expected project completion time can be computed from this path.

## 2. Six Steps in the Critical Path Method

There are six steps in the analysis of a network diagram using the Critical Path Method. They will be thoroughly discussed in this section.

### 2.1 Identification of Project Activities

If we are given a project and are asked to plan a programme of work for it, the first step is to analyse the objective of the project. What are the activities that should be done in order to accomplish the project? Then we should list the activities on a piece of paper; the activities listed may not necessarily be in a proper order. This is just a brainstorming exercise. (See Table 10.1 of Chapter 10.)

## 2.2 Network Formulation

Next, label the activities listed in Step 1 and then determine a logical sequence for the activities and form a network diagram for the list. The techniques involved were discussed in Chapter 10.

## 2.3 Duration Estimation

Then, based on individual experience, estimate the time duration $(t_e)$ of each activity in the network. Let us use Example 1 in Chapter 10 as an illustration. Suppose the estimated time durations, $t_e$, for the activities are as shown in Table 11.1.

| Activity | Description | $t_e$ (in days) |
|---|---|---|
| 1-2 | Obtain material | 1/2 |
| 1-3 | Obtain mixer | 1 |
| 1-4 | Dig hole 1 | 1 |
| 2-3 | (Dummy) | 0 |
| 4-5 | Dig hole 2 | 1 |
| 3-6 | Mix concrete | 1/4 |
| 4-7 | Set up pylon 1 | 3/4 |
| 5-8 | Set up pylon 2 | 3/4 |
| 6-7 | (Dummy) | 0 |
| 6-8 | (Dummy) | 0 |
| 7-9 | Concreting of pylon 1 by pouring concrete into hole 1 | 1/4 |
| 8-9 | Concreting of pylon 2 by pouring concrete into hole 2 | 1/4 |

**Table 11.1** Estimated time durations of the activities.

So now the estimated time durations can be put onto the network diagram (Fig. 11.1), which is similar to Fig. 10.11 of Chapter 10.

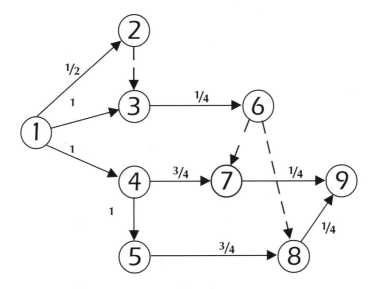

**Fig. 11.1** Network with estimated time durations.

## 2.4 Forward Pass Computation

This step involves the computation of the earliest start time of each activity. The computation process is called the **forward pass**.

The earliest start time is the earliest possible time by which the activity under consideration can be completed. That is to say, it is the time by which all the preceding activities merging into the start node of the activity have been completed.

To assist computation, the earliest start time (the result of the forward pass computation) is entered in a small square box beside each node, as shown in Fig. 11.2.

To calculate the earliest start time for an activity in a network, start with the start node with the smallest node number (the initial activity). Set this to zero (see Fig. 11.3). This means that activity 1-2 starts at zero time. This activity can be completed in half a day, so 1/2 is entered into the square next to node 2 (i.e. end node of activity 1-2 or start node of dummy activity 2-3).

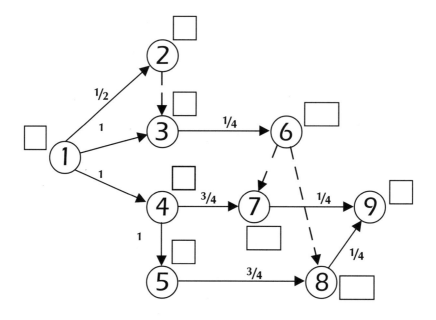

**Fig. 11.2**   Square boxes are put beside the nodes for entry of
earliest start times.

So, in general, add the $t_e$ of an activity to the figure in the square at the tail of
the arrow (i.e. start node) and put the sum in the square at the head of the
arrow (i.e. end node).

Let us consider some more examples. The $t_e$ of activity 1-4 is 1; hence we put
1 (0 + 1 = 1) in the square box next to node 4. The $t_e$ of activity 4-5 is also 1,
so we put 2 (1 + 1 = 2) in the box next to node 5.

Now let us consider activities which merge into a single node. Both activities
1-3 and 2-3 merge to node 3. Taking the path 1-2-3, node 3 can be reached
in 1/2 day because activity 2-3 has zero time duration, but when path 1-3 is
taken, node 3 can only be reached in 1 day. In this case, the *larger* figure
prevails. That is, 1 is put in the box beside node 3 instead of 1/2. This means
that activity 3-6 can only commence one day the earliest after the start of the
project.

Using this method, the earliest start time for all activities can be computed.
The earliest start time of an activity is the figure in the square box next to the
start node of that activity.

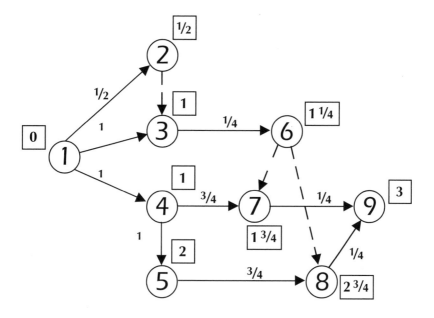

**Fig. 11.3**   Network with earliest start times.

Note that the earliest start time represented in the square box next to the last node (node 9 in this example) represents the duration of the project. In this example, the project duration is three days.

Before reading further, check that the computations in Fig. 11.3 are correct.

## 2.5   Backward Pass Computation

While the forward-pass computations provide us with the earliest start time of each activity the **backward pass** computations provide us with the **latest finish time** of the activity. The latest finish time is the latest possible time by which an activity must be completed if there is to be no delay in the completion of the project.

We usually draw a small circle beside each node for entry of the results of the backward pass computation (Fig. 11.4).

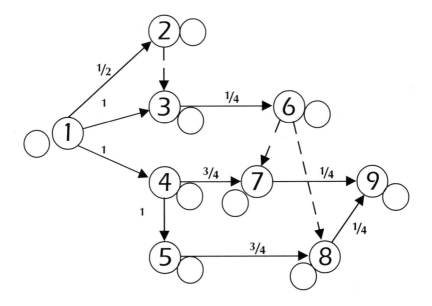

**Fig. 11.4** Network with circles for the entry of latest finish times.

In the backward-pass computation, we start with the last node (i.e., node 9 in this case).

The latest finish time of the last activity is equal to the project duration found from the forward-pass computation.

So 3 is put inside the circle next to node 9 (Fig. 11.5). Then the duration of the preceding activity is subtracted from this and the difference is put in the circle next to the preceding node. For example, the $t_e$ of activity 8-9 is $1/4$. We put $2^3/_4$ (i.e., $3 - 1/_4 = 2^3/_4$) in the circle next to node 8. The $t_e$ of activity 5-8 is 3/4; so we put 2 (i.e. $2^3/_4 - 3/_4 = 2$) in the circle next to node 5. This means that if the project is to be completed without delay, the latest finish time of activity 5-8 is $2^3/_4$ days after the project starts; the latest finish time of activity 4-5 is two days from the commencement date of the project and so on.

Now consider the situation where more than one activity proceeds from a node. Let us take the example of node 4. Activities 4-5 and 4-7 proceed from node 4. Taking path 4-5, the latest finish time for node 4 is 1, but when the path 4-7 is taken, the latest finish time at node 4 is 2. In such a case, the smaller figure is chosen. That is, 1 is put inside the circle beside node 4 instead of 2.

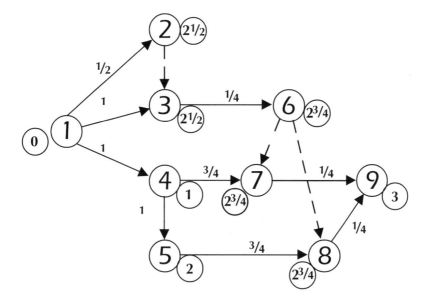

**Fig. 11.5**   Network with latest finish times.

Using this method, the latest finish times for each activity (i.e., represented by the circle next to the end node of the activity) can be computed.

Note that the figure in the circle next to the initial node is always zero.

Before reading further, check that the computations in Fig. 11.5 are correct.

## 2.6   Tracing the Critical Path

In Step 4, the project duration time is found by forward pass computation. There is a path which determines the shortest project duration. This **longest path** in the network, which also represents the **shortest project duration**, is called the **critical path**. Any delay in an activity which lies on the critical path will result in a delay of the project.

Comparing the networks in Figs. 11.3 and 11.5 shows that some nodes have earliest start times equal to the latest finish times. (See Fig. 11.6 which combines Figs. 11.3 and 11.5.) Others, however, have different figures. In the former case, the earliest start time of an activity represented by the start node which can be possibly achieved is the same as the latest finish time for the preceding activity (the same node representing the end node of that preceding activity) to be completed in order not to delay the overall schedule.

The case is therefore critical since there must be no delay between its achievement and the start of the next activity. By a similar argument, therefore, the critical path must pass through all nodes which have the same figures in their respective square and circle boxes.

The critical path is traced from the starting node through a series of nodes each of which has the earliest start time equal to the latest finish time. The critical path contains the series of activities which defines the project duration.

In our present example, the critical path is therefore given by 1-4-5-8-9. It can be seen that this is the path with the longest duration. Activities along this path (i.e. 1-4, 4-5, 5-8, 8-9) are called **critical activities** while all other activities are called **non-critical activities**.

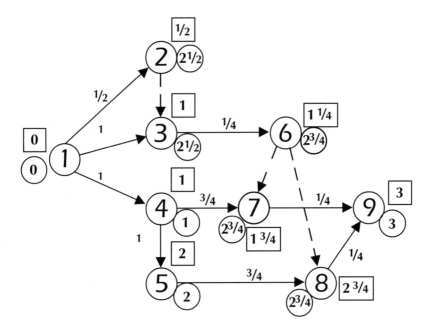

**Fig. 11.6**  Tracing the critical path.

## 3. The Float of an Activity

In Fig. 11.5, we have seen that the activities given in Table 11.2 form the critical path.

| Activity | Description | $t_e$ (in days) |
|----------|-------------|-----------------|
| 1-4 | Dig hole 1 | 1 |
| 4-5 | Dig hole 2 | 1 |
| 5-8 | Set up pylon 2 | 3/4 |
| 8-9 | Concreting of pylon 2 | 1/4 |

**Table 11.2**  Critical Activities of the Example.

These activities are critical activities which make up the overall project duration. They must be very well controlled in the process of construction because the completion of the project will be delayed if any one of them is delayed.

Delays of non-critical activities, however, may not affect the overall project completion. Let us now look into this point in more detail.

If we draw the critical activities along a time axis in days (Fig. 11.7), we get what is known as the critical activity chain, the duration of which is exactly equal to the time required for project completion (in this case three days).

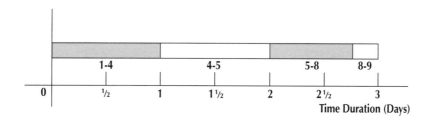

**Fig. 11.7**  Critical path chain: paths of critical activities drawn along a time axis.

There are other paths joining the starting node to the finishing node which are non-critical in the network (Fig. 11.6). They are listed below:

Path  1:     1-3-6-7-9
Path  2:     1-3-6-8-9
Path  3:     1-2-3-6-7-9
Path  4.     1-2-3-6-8-9
Path  5:     1-4-7-9

Let us now examine Path 2 (i.e. 1-3-6-8-9) and see how it relates to the critical path.

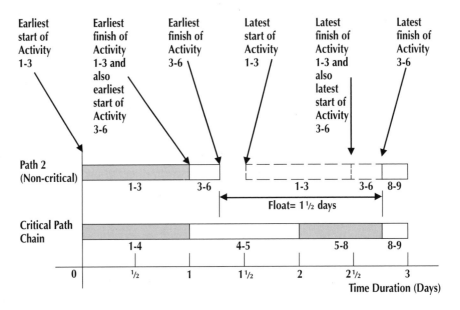

**Fig. 11.8**  Paths of all critical and some non-critical activities drawn along a time axis.

Some activities in Path 2 (i.e., 1-3 and 3-6) do not represent activities on the critical path but some (e.g. activity 8-9) form part of the critical path.

Let us consider activity 3-6, which lies entirely outside the critical path.

Associated with each activity is its latest finish time (given at the end of the activity) and its earliest start time (given at the start of that activity). The latest finish time of activity 3-6 is $2^3/_4$ days (indicated at node 6) and its earliest start time is 1 day (indicated at node 3). We do not know the earliest finish time of activity 3-6, but this is easy to find. If the activity commences at the earliest start time, then it will arrive at its earliest finish time after the duration of the activity. That is to say:

$$\text{Earliest finish time of an activity} = \text{Earliest start time of an activity} + \text{Duration of the activity}$$

The earliest finish time of activity 3-6 is therefore $1 + ^1/_4 = 1^1/_4$ days.

Now we define the difference between the latest finish time and earliest finish time of an activity to be the float of that activity. The float indicates the spare time or leeway for an activity. Such a float time is not available along the critical path. In the above example, activity 3-6 has a float $2\frac{3}{4}$ - $1\frac{1}{4}$ = $1\frac{1}{2}$ days. We can see that delay in the completion of the activities along a non-critical path within the float available will not affect the overall completion time of the project.

This statement may be written:

$$\text{Float} \quad = \quad \begin{matrix}\text{Latest finish time} \\ \text{of an activity}\end{matrix} \quad - \quad \begin{matrix}\text{Earliest finish time} \\ \text{of an activity}\end{matrix}$$

The latest start time is again easy to find. It is the latest time to start an activity so that the activity finishes at its latest finish time. That is to say:

$$\begin{matrix}\text{Latest start time} \\ \text{of an activity}\end{matrix} \quad = \quad \begin{matrix}\text{Latest finish time} \\ \text{of an activity}\end{matrix} \quad - \quad \begin{matrix}\text{Duration} \\ \text{of the activity}\end{matrix}$$

The latest start time of activity 3-6 is therefore $2\frac{3}{4} - \frac{1}{4} = 2\frac{1}{2}$ days.

In summary, the float of an activity can be found by:

either   (i)  Float = Latest Start Time   – Earliest Start Time
or      (ii) Float = Latest Finish Time – Earliest Finish Time

The readers can verify the following statements by themselves:

(i)  float of a critical activity = 0;   and
(ii) float of a non-critical activity > 0

Let us consider activity 3-6 and see how we actually calculate its float. As explained in the backward-pass computation in Section 11.2, the figure in the circle at node 6 (i.e., $2\frac{3}{4}$) is the latest finish time of activity 3-6. Also, as explained in the forward pass computation, the figure in the square at node 3 (i.e., 1) is the earliest start time of the activity.

However, the float of an activity is the difference between the latest finish time and the earliest finish time. And the earliest finish time can be found by just adding the duration of the activity to the earliest start time.

In general then, the float of an activity i-j can be computed as follows:

$(Float)_{i-j}$ = (Latest finish time of i-j) – (Earliest finish time of i-j)

= (Latest finish time of i-j) – (Earliest start time of i-j + Duration of i-j $(t_e)$)

= ( $\bigcirc$ of node j) – ( $\square$ of node i + $t_e$ of activity i-j)

The float of activity 3-6 is therefore: $(2\,^3/_4) – (1 + \,^1/_4) = 1\,^1/_2$ days.

## 4. Presenting Activities in a Bar Chart

After analysing a network using the critical path method, the activities of a project can be presented in a bar chart. The example in Section 11.2 will be used to illustrate this. Fig. 11.9 is a bar chart representing the activities of the project under consideration.

| Activity | Description | Days | | |
|---|---|---|---|---|
| | | 1 | 2 | 3 |
| 1-2 | Obtain material | | | |
| 1-3 | Obtain mixer | | | |
| 1-4 | Dig hole 1 | | | |
| 4-5 | Dig hole 2 | | | |
| 3-6 | Mix concrete | | | |
| 4-7 | Set up pylon 1 | | | |
| 5-8 | Set up pylon 2 | | | |
| 7-9 | Concreting of pylon 1 | | | |
| 8-9 | Concreting of pylon 2 | | | |

**Fig. 11.9** Bar chart indicating the schedule of the activities and their floats.

Note that all non-critical activities have been assumed to be carried out at their respective earliest start times. Floats of the activities are indicated on the chart. Note also that critical activities have no floats.

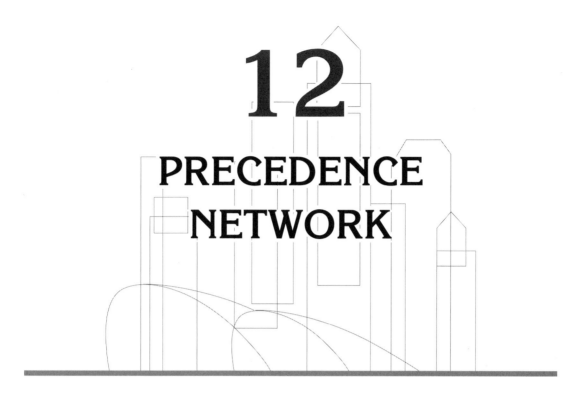

# 12

# PRECEDENCE NETWORK

## 1. Introduction

There is a second method that can be used to represent the activities in a project network. It is called a **precedence network** and has a number of advantages over the activity-on-arrow network we used in Chapters 10 and 11.

We shall now examine in detail how such a network is drawn.

## 2. Precedence Network Diagram

In all the previous discussions about critical path networks, we have used an arrow with a start node at its tail and an end node at its head to represent an activity, i.e.,

That is called an activity-on-arrow network. In this section, a new method of representing an activity is introduced. A node, instead of an arrow, is used to denote an activity. A network drawn in such manner is called a **precedence network** (or **activity-on-node** network). For example,

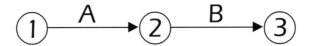

in an activity-on-arrow network would be represented as:

in a precedence network. Let us now look at a few more examples (Fig. 12.1):

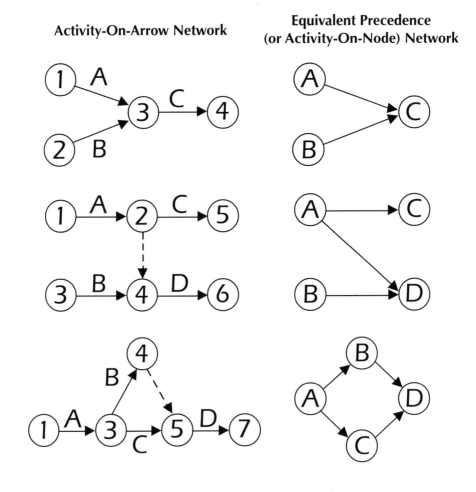

**Fig. 12.1** Examples of equivalent networks.

From the above examples in Fig. 12.1, it can be seen that the precedence networks have several advantages over the activity-on-arrow (or AOA) networks. These include:

1. No dummy activity is necessary in a precedence network.
2. A precedence network is usually simpler than an AOA network for the same number of activities, because there are no dummies.
3. In a precedence network, each activity can be assigned a single unique number to represent it; but in an AOA network, an activity has to be represented by two numbers, i and j. Hence, the creation and modification (addition or deletion of activities) of a precedence network diagram is easier.
4. Less arithmetic will be involved in the forward pass and backward pass in a precedence network since there are no dummies.

Let us now look at the following example which uses a precedence network diagram instead of AOA diagram to represent a project. The AOA network is shown in Fig. 12.2. Fig. 12.3 shows the equivalent precedence network which represents the same project.

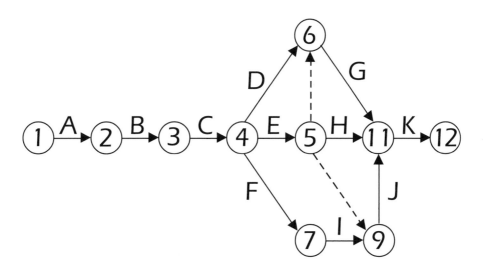

**Fig. 12.2**   The AOA network.

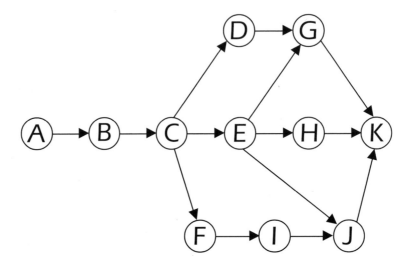

**Fig. 12.3**   An equivalent precedence network.

We can see that each node in the precedence network now represents an activity. The arrows no longer represent activities. The arrows just show the logic of the network (i.e. the sequence of the activities).

### 3.   Forward and Backward Passes Using Precedence Network

The forward and backward passes in network analysis can be done using a precedence network, which provides a simpler representation. Four steps are involved.

### 3.1   Drawing the Network

In this first step, Fig. 12.3 is redrawn so that each node in the network is changed into a square which is subdivided into compartments, as shown in Fig. 12.4. The activity label is put inside the central compartment of the square.

**Legend :-**

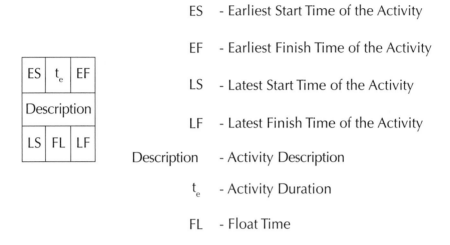

ES    - Earliest Start Time of the Activity

EF    - Earliest Finish Time of the Activity

LS    - Latest Start Time of the Activity

LF    - Latest Finish Time of the Activity

Description    - Activity Description

$t_e$    - Activity Duration

FL    - Float Time

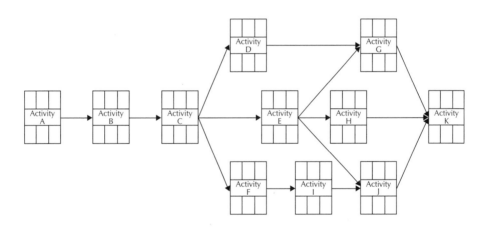

**Fig. 12.4**   Precedence network with nodes each having seven compartments.

## 3.2    Putting in the Activity Durations

In the second step, the activity duration is placed in the top central compartment of the square, as shown in Fig. 12.5.

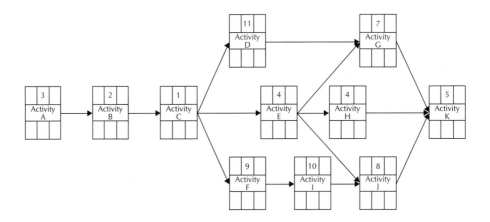

**Fig. 12.5**    Precedence network with durations placed in the top central compartment.

## 3.3    Forward and Backward Pass Computations

The third step is to carry out the forward pass and backward pass computation. So the earliest start time of each activity is calculated and is written in the top left compartment of each square, as shown in Fig. 12.6. The method of carrying out forward pass computation is similar to that described in section 2 of Chapter 11.

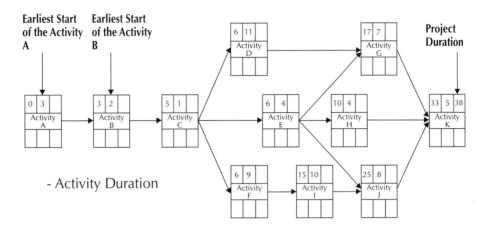

**Fig. 12.6** Precedence network with durations and earliest start times.

The backward pass computation gives the latest finish time of each activity and this is written in the bottom right compartment of each square, as shown in Fig. 12.7. Again the method of computation is similar to that described in section 2 of Chapter 11.

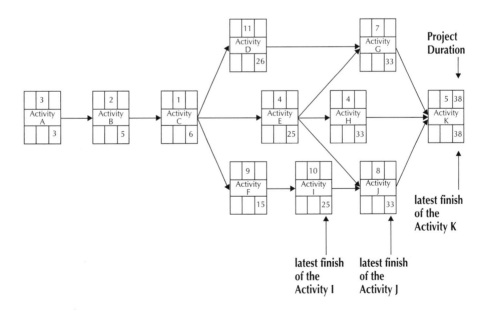

**Fig. 12.7** Precedence network with durations and latest finish times.

The complete precedence network with the earliest start times and the latest finish times is shown in Fig. 12.8.

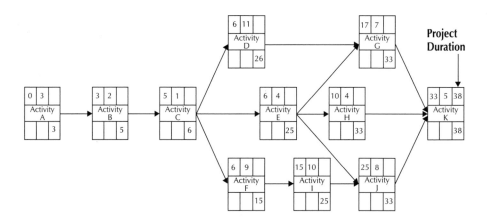

**Fig. 12.8** Precedence network with durations, earliest start times and latest finish times.

## 3.4 Tracing the Critical Path

In order to complete all boxes in the network, the earliest finish time, the latest start time and the float of each activity are calculated and entered into the boxes, as shown Fig. 12.9.

Then the critical path can be traced using the method described before (see section 2 in Chapter 11). The critical activity has its earliest start time equal to its latest start time (i.e. float = 0). In our case, activities A, B, C, F, I, J and K are critical activities. Hence the critical path is: A-B-C-F-I-J-K.

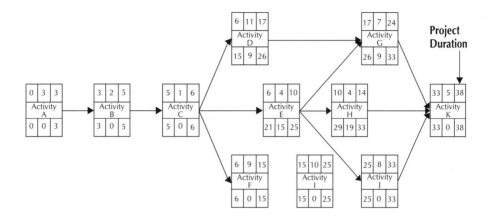

**Fig. 12.9** Complete precedence network.

## 4.   Overlapping Activities and Lead-Time Relationships

For a precedence or AON diagram, it is possible to allow overlapping relationship between any two activities. For example, if activity I, in Fig. 12. 9, can commence 6 days after the commencement of activity F, then we say that activity F and I are overlapping activities, because activity I does not have to wait for activity F ($t_e$ = 9 days) to finish before its commencement. We usually refer to such a case as an SS (start-to-start) relationship, and in this case, $SS_{FI}$ is 6 days. The $SS_{FI}$ relationship is drawn in a manner as shown in Fig. 12.10.

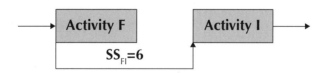

**Fig. 12.10**   SS (start-to-start) relationship.

There are three more 'lead-time' relationships besides the SS relationship:

- FF (finish-to-finish) relationship
- FS (finish-to-start) relationship
- SF (start-to-finish) relationship

These relationships are drawn in the ways as shown in Fig. 12.11.

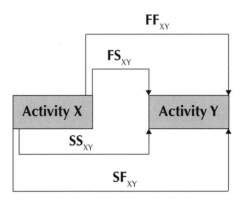

**Fig. 12.11**   SS, FF, FS and SF relationships in a precedence network.

The methods in computing the forward and backward passes for SS, FF, FS and SF relationships can be found in Chapter 7 of the second edition of *Project Management: Techniques in Planning and Controlling Construction Projects* by H.N. Ahuja *et al.* (1994). These methods are not discussed in this chapter as the author has reservation on the use of these 'lead-time' relationships, because they may cause inconsistent results and confusions, especially when a network is large.

G.D. Oberlender has documented in Chapter 8 of the second edition of his book *Project Management for Engineering and Construction* (2000) the reasons and examples on the inconsistency and confusion in using the 'lead-time' relationships for precedence diagrams. He also recommends that the use of a pure (conventional) precedence network (or pure AON network), as described in this chapter, should be promoted. A precedence network containing 'lead-time' relationships can be converted to a pure AON network without those relationships by simply adding additional activities. The conversion procedure is simple and an example is shown in Fig. 12.12. More examples can be found in Oberlender's book. Although additional activities may appear as a disadvantage, yet adding activities provides a clear understanding of the sequence of work, thus preventing confusion and misunderstanding of the project schedule, as is opined by Oberlender. The author of this chapter agrees with his view.

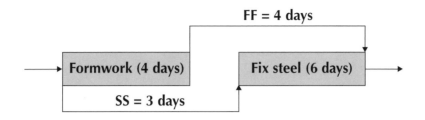

**Fig. 12.12a**   Network with SS and FF relationships.

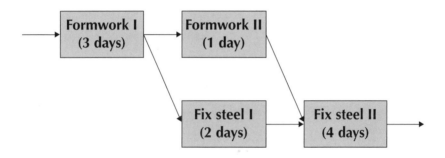

**Fig. 12.12b**   The same network without SS and FF relationships but with additional activities.

# 13

# PERT AND ITS PROBABILITY CONCEPT

## 1. What Is PERT?

The full name of PERT is Programme Evaluation and Review Technique. It is the application of the critical path method to calculate project duration with uncertainty. The critical path method that has been introduced in Chapters 11 and 12 involves the assignment of activity duration for every activity involved. This is done by estimating single activity duration based on past experience. Besides that, to determine activity duration, a method known as PERT can also be used and this involves probabilities.

PERT uses three quantities in estimating the duration of a single activity:

1. the optimistic time
2. the pessimistic time
3. the most likely time

The critical path method (CPM) and the PERT were developed independently in 1957, but they have a lot in common. Both make use of a network diagram and use critical path analysis to represent and analyse a project. The main difference between CPM and PERT is that CPM uses only a single time estimate for an activity. PERT is usually applied to projects which are carried out under considerable uncertainty and is used to predict the probability of completion of a certain project within a certain period of time. This will be discussed in more detail in the next section.

## 2.    The Probability Concept of PERT

It is empirical that when an activity is repeating many times, the activity durations recorded will follow a β-distribution. Fig. 13.1 shows a typical β-distribution curve.

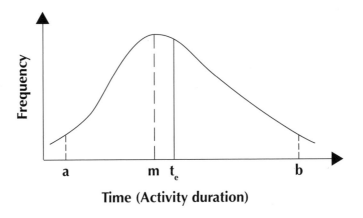

**Time (Activity duration)**

**Fig. 13.1**    A β-distribution curve.

The terms a, b, and m shown on the curve in Fig.13.1 are defined below:

a = the optimistic time, i.e. the shortest duration which could be anticipated for the activity

b = the pessimistic time, i.e. the duration of the activity when everything takes a long time to complete

m = the most likely time

Note that the optimistic and pessimistic times could only occur once every hundred times. Hence, three two vertical lines (i.e. a and b) divide the area under the β-curve into the ratio of 1:99.

In PERT, the activity duration time $t_e$ of an activity is given by the **expected time** or **mean time** required to complete the activity. It can be shown (though the proof is outside the scope of this book) that:

$$t_e = \frac{a + 4m + b}{6}$$

Notice that the vertical line through $t_e$ in th β-curve divides the area under the curve into two equal halves.

The standard deviation (σ) and the variance ($σ^2$) of the β-distribution are given by:

$$σ = \frac{b - a}{6}$$

and

$$σ^2 = (\frac{b - a}{6})^2$$

Although the duration of an individual activity follows a β-distribution, the completion time for a series of activities in a chain takes the form of a normal distribution (this is also empirical). Fig. 13.2 shows this curve. Notice that the vertical line at $T_e$, which is the expected project completion time, divides the area under the normal distribution curve into two equal halves.

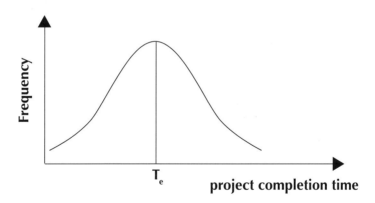

**Fig. 13.2**   The normal distribution for the project completion time. $T_e$ is the expected project completion time.

## 3.    Example of a PERT Problem

The following network diagram shows the sequence of a project.

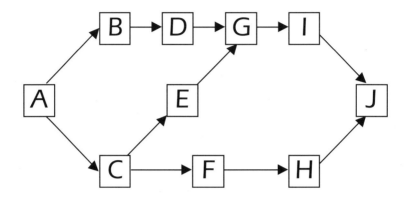

**Fig. 13.3** The network diagram of the project.

The optimistic, the most likely and the pessimistic time estimates in weeks for each activity are given in Table 13.1.

| Activity | Duration | | |
|:---:|:---:|:---:|:---:|
| | Optimistic (a) | Most likely (m) | Pessimistic (b) |
| A | 4 | 6 | 9 |
| B | 3 | 6 | 8 |
| C | 7 | 10 | 12 |
| D | 1 | 2 | 4 |
| E | 3 | 6 | 10 |
| F | 2 | 5 | 7 |
| G | 7 | 9 | 11 |
| H | 4 | 8 | 10 |
| I | 5 | 7 | 9 |
| J | 5 | 8 | 10 |

**Table 13.1** Optimistic, most likely and the pessimistic durations for the activities.

Determine the probability that the project can be completed in 48 weeks.

Solution

Firstly, determine the mean duration ($t_e$) of the activities.

| Activity | a | m | b | $t_e$ |
|:---:|:---:|:---:|:---:|:---:|
| A | 4 | 6 | 9 | $\dfrac{4 + 4 \times 6 + 9}{6} = 6\dfrac{1}{6}$ |
| B | 3 | 6 | 8 | $\dfrac{3 + 4 \times 6 + 8}{6} = 5\dfrac{5}{6}$ |
| C | 7 | 10 | 12 | $\dfrac{7 + 4 \times 10 + 12}{6} = 9\dfrac{5}{6}$ |
| D | 1 | 2 | 4 | $\dfrac{1 + 4 \times 2 + 4}{6} = 2\dfrac{1}{6}$ |
| E | 3 | 6 | 10 | $\dfrac{3 + 4 \times 6 + 10}{6} = 6\dfrac{1}{6}$ |
| F | 2 | 5 | 7 | $\dfrac{2 + 4 \times 5 + 7}{6} = 4\dfrac{5}{6}$ |
| G | 7 | 9 | 11 | $\dfrac{7 + 4 \times 9 + 11}{6} = 9$ |
| H | 4 | 8 | 10 | $\dfrac{4 + 4 \times 8 + 10}{6} = 7\dfrac{4}{6}$ |
| I | 5 | 7 | 9 | $\dfrac{5 + 4 \times 7 + 9}{6} = 7$ |
| J | 5 | 8 | 10 | $\dfrac{5 + 4 \times 8 + 10}{6} = 7\dfrac{5}{6}$ |

**Table 13.2** Optimistic, most likely, pessimistic durations and $t_e$ for the activities.

The network with necessary computations is :

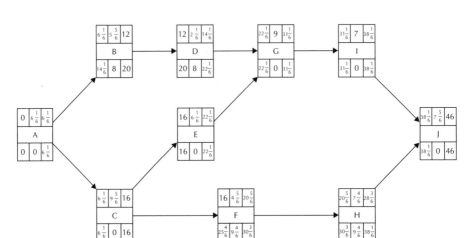

**Fig. 13.3** The network diagram showing calculations.

Critical path: A-C-E-G-I-J and the project duration $T_e$ is 46 weeks.

| Critical Activities | Standard Deviation (σ) | variance (σ²) |
|:---:|:---:|:---:|
| A | $\dfrac{9-4}{6} = \dfrac{5}{6}$ | $\dfrac{25}{36}$ |
| C | $\dfrac{12-7}{6} = \dfrac{5}{6}$ | $\dfrac{25}{36}$ |
| E | $\dfrac{10-3}{6} = \dfrac{7}{6}$ | $\dfrac{49}{36}$ |
| G | $\dfrac{11-7}{6} = \dfrac{4}{6}$ | $\dfrac{16}{36}$ |
| I | $\dfrac{9-5}{6} = \dfrac{4}{6}$ | $\dfrac{16}{36}$ |
| J | $\dfrac{10-5}{6} = \dfrac{5}{6}$ | $\dfrac{25}{36}$ |
| | Total | $\dfrac{156}{36}$ |

**Table 13.3** Standard deviations and variances of the critical activities.

It is assumed that the variance of completion time of a chain of activities is equal to the sum of the variances of the individual activities in the chain.

$\therefore$ Variance of project duration $= \dfrac{156}{36} = \dfrac{13}{3}$

Hence the standard deviation of the project duration $= \sqrt{\dfrac{13}{3}} = 2.082$

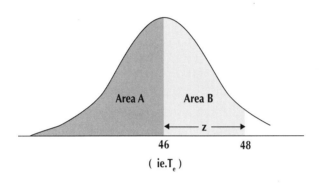

**Fig. 13.4** Normal distribution of project completion time $T_e$.

Now the expected (or mean) project duration is 46 weeks and the standard deviation is 2.082 weeks.

To find the probability of completing the project within 48 weeks, we have to find the shaded area shown in Fig. 13.4.

To find the area B, first we have to find the normal variate z.

$$z = \frac{48 - 46}{2.082} = 0.9608$$

From the normal distribution statistical table,

if $z = 0.9608$, then Area B $=$ 0.331

| Total area shaded | $=$ | Area A + Area B |
| | $=$ | 0.5 + 0.331 |
| | $=$ | 0.831 (i.e., 83.1%) |

$\therefore$ The probability that the project can be completed in 48 weeks is 83.1%.

# 14

# TIME-COST OPTIMIZATION OF A PROJECT

## 1.   Theory of Time-Cost Optimization

If an activity is to be completed sooner than its normal duration $(t_e)$, the cost is usually higher because extra resources must be put into the activity.

A typical time-cost curve generally tends to concave upwards as shown in Fig. 14.1.

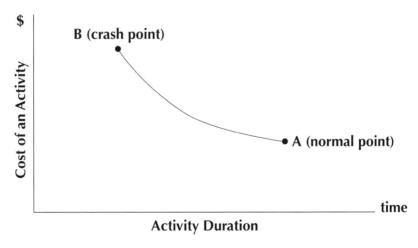

**Fig. 14.1**   Time-cost curve for an activity.

As the activity is speeded up, costs will go up until Point B is reached.

Point B is the shortest possible time for completing the activity. This is called the crash point.

When the crash point is reached, further attempts to shorten the duration time by employing additional resources would only increase the cost but would not shorten the time of completion.

To simplify costing, the time-cost curve is assumed to be a straight line for an activity, as shown in Fig.14.2.

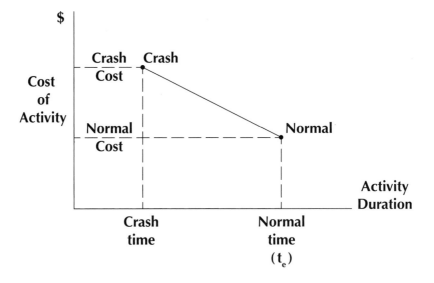

**Fig. 14.2**  Simplified time-cost curve (straight line relationship) of an activity.

The slope of the line would represent the cost to shorten the activity by one day. The slope is called the **cost slope** (usually denoted by C).

$$\text{Cost slope (C)} \ = \ \frac{\text{Crash cost} - \text{Normal cost}}{\text{Crash time} - \text{Normal time}} \ = \ \$/\text{day to shorten an activity}$$

A project usually consists of many activities. If a time-cost curve of the duration of a project is plotted, it is also a concave upward curve, like a single activity curve, as shown in Fig. 14.3 (see curve P) while the magnitude of the cost ($) and the duration (time) is much greater in the project curve than in the activity curve. Note that a project time-cost curve, unlike an activity time-cost curve, cannot be simplified as a straight line.

Although the **direct cost** of the project (curve P) rises as the completion time is shortened, the **indirect cost** (curve Q) will fall as the project duration decreases (indirect cost usually refers to overheads). If the total of the direct and indirect costs (curve R) is plotted against time, there is a minimum point in the total cost curve R, as shown in Fig. 14.3.

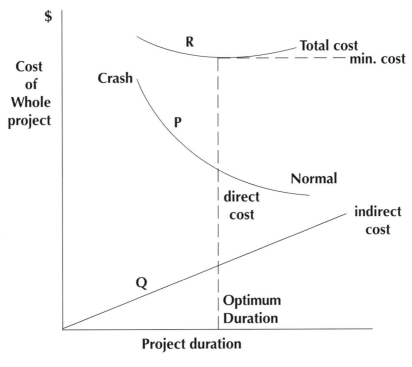

**Fig. 14.3**  Time-cost optimization curve for a project.

## 2.  **Example of Time-Cost Optimization of a Small Project**

Fig.14.4 shows a small project with seven activities.

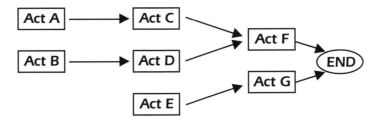

**Fig. 14.4**  Network diagram.

The normal duration and cost and the crash duration and cost of each activity are as follows:

| Activity | Normal | | Crash | |
|---|---|---|---|---|
| | Duration (days) | Cost ($) | Duration (days) | Cost ($) |
| A | 5 | 100 | 4 | 120 |
| B | 4 | 150 | 3 | 170 |
| C | 3 | 150 | 3 | 150 |
| D | 6 | 300 | 4 | 400 |
| E | 2 | 200 | 2 | 200 |
| F | 9 | 550 | 5 | 990 |
| G | 3 | 100 | 2 | 150 |
| | | $\Sigma=1550$ | | $\Sigma=2180$ |

**Table 14.1**  The normal duration and cost and the crash duration and cost of each activity.

Assuming an indirect cost of $60/day, determine the optimal project duration.

To find the optimal project duration, we follow a four-step approach as shown below.

## Step 1

Carry out, using normal duration, the forward and backward passes and hence identify the critical path.

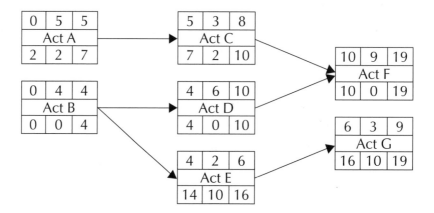

**Fig. 14.5**  Precedence diagram.

The critical path is B-D-F.

## Step 2

Find the differences in cost and duration of 'crash' and 'normal' of each and every activity in the network and hence the cost slope (C) of each activity.

| Activity | Difference in cost ($) | Difference in duration (day) | C ($/day) |
|----------|------------------------|------------------------------|-----------|
| A | 20 | 1 | 20 |
| B | 20 | 1 | 20 |
| C | - | - | - |
| D | 100 | 2 | 50 |
| E | - | - | - |
| F | 440 | 4 | 110 |
| G | 50 | 1 | 50 |

**Table 14.2** The differences in 'crash' and 'normal' cost and duration and the cost slope (C) of each activity.

## Step 3

First, draw a table similar to Table 14.3.

| Activity | C ($/day) | Duration shortened (day) | Cost of shortening ($) | New project cost ($) | New project duration (day) |
|----------|-----------|--------------------------|------------------------|----------------------|----------------------------|
|  |  |  |  |  |  |
|  |  |  |  |  |  |
|  |  |  |  |  |  |

**Table 14.3** Time-cost optimization (1).

Begin shortening with a critical activity because the project duration can be shortened only if a critical activity is shortened and it is of no use to shorten a non-critical activity. There are, however, three critical activities: B, D and F. Which one should we shorten first? We should shorten the critical activity with the lowest cost slope C, that is, activity B in our example, because we want to make the project time-cost curve a concave upward curve. So, we can firstly fill in the table as follows:

| Activity | C ($/day) | Duration shortened (day) | Cost of shortening ($) | New project cost ($) | New project duration (day) |
|----------|-----------|--------------------------|------------------------|----------------------|----------------------------|
| B | 20 | 1 | 20 | $1,550 + 20 = 1,570$ | $19 - 1 = 18$ |

Table 14.4   Time-cost optimization (2).

The next step is to shorten another critical activity. This time we shorten the remaining critical activity with the lowest cost slope C, and it is activity D which now has the lowest C. Since activity D can be shortened by 2 days, we continue to fill in the table as follows:

| Activity | C ($/day) | Duration shortened (day) | Cost of shortening ($) | New project cost ($) | New project duration (day) |
|----------|-----------|--------------------------|------------------------|----------------------|----------------------------|
| B | 20 | 1 | 20 | $1,550 + 20 = 1,570$ | $19 - 1 = 18$ |
| D | 50 | 2 | 100 | $1,570 + 100 = 1,670$ | $18 - 2 = 16$ |

Table 14.5   Time-cost optimization (3).

Is the above shortening correct?

If we look at the project network again, we can see that there are three paths in the network, namely, A-C-F, B-D-F and B-E-G. Originally, the critical path B-D-F takes 19 days to complete before activities B and D are shortened; it now takes 16 days to complete after activity B is shortened by 1 day and activity D is shortened by 2 days. If we look at path A-C-F which originally takes 17 days to complete, now it still needs 17 days to complete because the shortening of activities B and C does not at all affect the time of completion. Now, B-D-F takes 16 days to complete and A-C-F takes 17 days to complete. This means that the critical path has been re-routed from B-D-F to A-C-F and the project duration is not 16 days (as shown in Table 14.5) but 17 days. The critical path becomes A-C-F; it is no longer B-D-F. Therefore, the new project duration of 16 days as shown in Table 14.5 is wrong.

It is important to note that when shortening a critical activity, it is necessary to check that another path does not become critical and the original critical path is therefore not re-routed through another series of activities.

In our example, what we have done in Table 14.5 is wrong. We should have shortened activity D by 1 day instead of 2 days (although activity D can at most be shortened by 2 days) such that two critical paths A-C-F and B-D-F would simultaneously occur and both paths take 17 days to complete. This is shown in Table 14.6.

| Activity | C ($/day) | Duration shortened (day) | Cost of shortening ($) | New project cost ($) | New project duration (day) |
|---|---|---|---|---|---|
| B | 20 | 1 | 20 | 1,550+20=1,570 | 19 – 1=18 |
| ~~D~~ | ~~50~~ | ~~2~~ | ~~100~~ | ~~1,570+100=1,670~~ | ~~18 – 2=16~~ |
| D | 50 | 1 | 50 | 1,570+50=1,620 | 18 – 1=17 |
| | | | | | |

**Table 14.6**   Time-cost optimization (4).

When another critical path is created, joint-shortening of durations of two activities, one in each critical path, is necessary. Care, in such circumstances, must be taken to select the lowest joint-cost. The figures in column C must be in increasing order so that the project time-cost curve is concave upward. This point will be further discussed later.

Next, we must shorten both activities A and D together by one day each. Activity A is on the critical path A-C-F and activity D (left behind 1 more day to shorten) is on the critical path B-D-F. Note that the joint-cost of A and D is the lowest at this stage. The joint-shortening is shown in Table 14.7.

| Activity | C ($/day) | Duration shortened (day) | Cost of shortening ($) | New project cost ($) | New project duration (day) |
|---|---|---|---|---|---|
| B | 20 | 1 | 20 | $1,550 + 20 = 1,570$ | $19 - 1 = 18$ |
| D | 50 | 1 | 50 | $1,570 + 50 = 1,620$ | $18 - 1 = 17$ |
| Two critical paths occur | | | | | |
| A + D | $20 + 50 = 70$ | 1 | 70 | $1,620 + 70 = 1,690$ | $17 - 1 = 16$ |

**Table 14.7**  Time-cost optimization (5).

Next, we shorten activity F by 4 days (from 9 days to 5 days). This is the only possible shortening left in the network. Further shortening (e.g. activity G) will only incur unnecessary costs but will not shorten the project duration. The shortest possible time to complete the project is 12 days, as shown in Table 14.8.

| Activity | C ($/day) | Duration shortened (day) | Cost of shortening ($) | New project cost ($) | New project duration (day) |
|---|---|---|---|---|---|
| B | 20 | 1 | 20 | $1,550 + 20 = 1,570$ | $19 - 1 = 18$ |
| D | 50 | 1 | 50 | $1,570 + 50 = 1,620$ | $18 - 1 = 17$ |
| Two critical paths occur | | | | | |
| A + D | $20 + 50 = 70$ | 1 | 70 | $1,620 + 70 = 1,690$ | $17 - 1 = 16$ |
| F | 110 | 4 | 440 | $1,690 + 440 = 2,130$ | $16 - 4 = 12$ |

**Table 14.8**  Time-cost optimization (6).

Now, the project duration reaches its crash point. The crash duration is 12 days. Note that the second column of Table 14.8 (C column) must be with C values in increasing order. This is to ensure that we will have a concave upward direct cost curve.

## Step 4

We can now draw the time-cost optimisation curve similar to the one in Fig. 14.3. The direct cost curve is plotted by the use of the figures in the last two columns of Table 14.8 in step 3. The indirect cost curve is plotted as a linear graph with a slope of $60/day (given). The total cost curve is drawn by summing up the y axis of the above two curves. The curves are shown in Fig. 14.6.

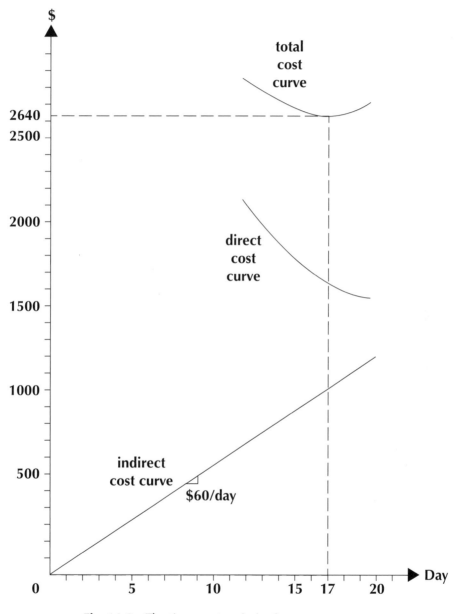

**Fig. 14.6**   The time-cost optimisation curve.

From Fig. 14.6, we can see that the optimal project duration is 17 days, and the optimal (minimum) total project cost is $2,640.

# 15

# CRITICAL PATH
# AND LINEAR
# PROGRAMMING

## 1. Critical Path of a Precedence Network

It is possible that the critical path of a precedence network be found by the use of linear programming techniques. The following example illustrates this.

### 1.1 Example

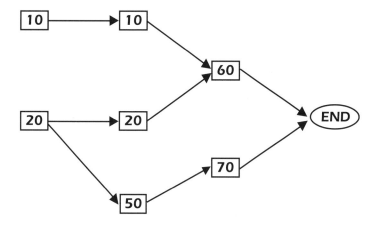

**Fig. 15.1** An activity-on-node network.

The durations of the activities of a project are shown in the network diagram in Fig. 15.1 and are as follows:

| Activity | Activity duration (weeks) |
|---|---|
| 10 | 5 |
| 20 | 4 |
| 30 | 3 |
| 40 | 6 |
| 50 | 2 |
| 60 | 9 |
| 70 | 3 |

Find the shortest project duration (critical path) by the use of linear programming.

## Solution

Let $x_{10}$ = start time of activity 10

$x_{20}$ = start time of activity 20

.

.

.

$x_{70}$ = start time of activity 70

$x_{END}$ = project duration

The objective is to:

Minimize $Z = x_{END}$

subject to

$$x_{30} - x_{10} \geq 5 \quad \text{............................................................}(1)$$

$$x_{40} - x_{20} \geq 4 \quad \text{............................................................}(2)$$

$$x_{50} - x_{20} \geq 4 \quad \text{............................................................}(3)$$

$$x_{60} - x_{30} \geq 3 \quad \text{............................................................}(4)$$

$$x_{60} - x_{40} \geq 6 \quad \dots\dots\dots\dots\dots\dots\dots\dots\dots\dots\dots\dots\dots\dots\dots\dots\dots \text{(5)}$$

$$x_{70} - x_{50} \geq 2 \quad \dots\dots\dots\dots\dots\dots\dots\dots\dots\dots\dots\dots\dots\dots\dots\dots\dots \text{(6)}$$

$$x_{END} - x_{60} \geq 9 \quad \dots\dots\dots\dots\dots\dots\dots\dots\dots\dots\dots\dots\dots\dots\dots\dots \text{(7)}$$

$$x_{END} - x_{70} \geq 3 \quad \dots\dots\dots\dots\dots\dots\dots\dots\dots\dots\dots\dots\dots\dots\dots\dots \text{(8)}$$

All $x_i \geq 0$    for i = 10, 20, 30, 40, 50, 60, 70, END

The solution for this model is:

Shortest project duration = minimum $x_{END}$ = 19 weeks

$$x_{10} = 2$$
$$x_{20} = 0$$
$$x_{30} = 7$$
$$x_{40} = 4$$
$$x_{50} = 14$$
$$x_{60} = 10$$
$$x_{70} = 16$$
$$x_{END} = 19$$

Readers can always check whether the project duration is 19 weeks or not using the critical path method.

## 2. Time-Cost Optimization of a Project Network

In the previous example, we have seen how the critical path or the shortest path in a project network can be found using the linear programming method. Now, we shall see how the time-cost optimisation can be done if the normal duration and cost and the crash duration and cost of each activity in the network are given.

### 2.1 Example

The normal duration and cost and those of the crash for the activities of the network in the previous example (Fig. 15.1) are as follows:

| Activity | Normal | | Crash | |
|---|---|---|---|---|
| | Duration (R) | Cost (U) | Duration (Q) | Cost (V) |
| 10 | 5 weeks | $100 | 4 weeks | $120 |
| 20 | 4 | 150 | 3 | 170 |
| 30 | 3 | 150 | 3 | 150 |
| 40 | 6 | 300 | 4 | 400 |
| 50 | 2 | 200 | 2 | 200 |
| 60 | 9 | 550 | 5 | 990 |
| 70 | 3 | 100 | 2 | 150 |

The indirect cost (overheads and so on) of the project is $60 per week. How should the activities be compressed so that an optimal project duration can be achieved with the minimum total direct and indirect costs of the project?

Solution

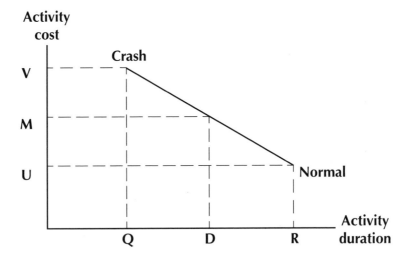

**Fig. 15.2** Definitions of M and D.

In Fig. 15.2, we denote the normal duration and crash duration by R and Q respectively, and normal cost and crash cost by U and V respectively.

The cost slope of an activity between normal and crash $= C = \dfrac{V-U}{R-Q}$

Now, we can calculate C of each activity:

| Activity | $C = \dfrac{V-U}{R-Q}$ |
|:---:|:---:|
| 10 | 20 |
| 20 | 20 |
| 30 | - |
| 40 | 50 |
| 50 | - |
| 60 | 110 |
| 70 | 50 |

An activity can be shortened to any duration between R and Q. We assume that D is the activity duration after compressing $(R \geq D \geq Q)$ such that the time and cost of the overall project is optimized. M is the corresponding cost associated with D.

By similar triangles, we can easily derive that

$$D = R - \frac{1}{C}(M - U)$$

Therefore, for each activity:

$$D_{10} = 5 - \frac{1}{20}(M_{10} - 100)$$

$$D_{20} = 4 - \frac{1}{20}(M_{20} - 150)$$

$$D_{30} = 3$$

$$D_{40} = 6 - \frac{1}{50}(M_{40} - 300)$$

$$D_{50} = 2$$

$$D_{60} = 9 - \frac{1}{110}(M_{60} - 550)$$

$$D_{70} = 3 - \frac{1}{50}(M_{70} - 100)$$

Using the formulation discussed in the example, the activity duration constraints are:

$$x_{30} - x_{10} \geq D_{10}$$    (Remember that $x_i$ is the

$$x_{40} - x_{20} \geq D_{20}$$    start time of activity i)

$$x_{50} - x_{50} \geq D_{20}$$

$$x_{60} - x_{30} \geq D_{30}$$

$$x_{60} - x_{40} \geq D_{40}$$

$$x_{70} - x_{50} \geq D_{50}$$

$$x_{END} - x_{60} \geq D_{60}$$

$$x_{END} - x_{70} \geq D_{70}$$

These can be written as:

$$x_{30} - x_{10} \geq 5 - \frac{1}{20}(M_{10} - 100) \quad \dots \dots \dots (1)$$

$$x_{40} - x_{20} \geq 4 - \frac{1}{20}(M_{20} - 150) \quad \dots \dots \dots (2)$$

$$x_{50} - x_{20} \geq 4 - \frac{1}{20}(M_{20} - 150) \quad \dots \dots \dots (3)$$

$$x_{60} - x_{30} \geq 3 \quad \dots \dots \dots (4)$$

$$x_{60} - x_{40} \geq 6 - \frac{1}{50}(M_{40} - 300) \quad \dots \dots \dots (5)$$

$$x_{70} - x_{50} \geq 2 \quad \dots \dots \dots (6)$$

$$x_{END} - x_{60} \geq 9 - \frac{1}{110}(M_{60} - 550) \quad \dots \dots \dots (7)$$

$$x_{END} - x_{70} \geq 3 - \frac{1}{50}(M_{70} - 100) \quad \dots \dots \dots (8)$$

The second set of constraints is the minimum cost (or normal cost) constraints:

$$M_{10} \geq 100 \quad \dots \dots \dots (9)$$

$$M_{20} \geq 150 \quad \dots \dots \dots (10)$$

$$M_{30} \geq 150 \quad \dots \dots \dots (11)$$

$$M_{40} \geq 300 \quad \dots \dots \dots (12)$$

$$M_{50} \geq 200 \qquad \dotsc\dotsc\dotsc\dotsc\dotsc\dotsc\dotsc\dotsc\dotsc\dotsc\dotsc\dotsc (13)$$

$$M_{60} \geq 550 \qquad \dotsc\dotsc\dotsc\dotsc\dotsc\dotsc\dotsc\dotsc\dotsc\dotsc\dotsc\dotsc (14)$$

$$M_{70} \geq 100 \qquad \dotsc\dotsc\dotsc\dotsc\dotsc\dotsc\dotsc\dotsc\dotsc\dotsc\dotsc\dotsc (15)$$

The third set of constraints is the maximum cost (or crash cost) constraints:

$$M_{10} \leq 120 \qquad \dotsc\dotsc\dotsc\dotsc\dotsc\dotsc\dotsc\dotsc\dotsc\dotsc\dotsc\dotsc (16)$$

$$M_{20} \leq 170 \qquad \dotsc\dotsc\dotsc\dotsc\dotsc\dotsc\dotsc\dotsc\dotsc\dotsc\dotsc\dotsc (17)$$

$$M_{30} \leq 150 \qquad \dotsc\dotsc\dotsc\dotsc\dotsc\dotsc\dotsc\dotsc\dotsc\dotsc\dotsc\dotsc (18)$$

$$M_{40} \leq 400 \qquad \dotsc\dotsc\dotsc\dotsc\dotsc\dotsc\dotsc\dotsc\dotsc\dotsc\dotsc\dotsc (19)$$

$$M_{50} \leq 200 \qquad \dotsc\dotsc\dotsc\dotsc\dotsc\dotsc\dotsc\dotsc\dotsc\dotsc\dotsc\dotsc (20)$$

$$M_{60} \leq 990 \qquad \dotsc\dotsc\dotsc\dotsc\dotsc\dotsc\dotsc\dotsc\dotsc\dotsc\dotsc\dotsc (21)$$

$$M_{70} \leq 150 \qquad \dotsc\dotsc\dotsc\dotsc\dotsc\dotsc\dotsc\dotsc\dotsc\dotsc\dotsc\dotsc (22)$$

Other constraints are:

$$M_i \geq 0 \qquad \text{for } i = 1, 2, \dotsc, 7$$

$$\text{and } x_i \geq 0 \qquad \text{for } i = 1, 2, \dotsc, 7, \text{END}$$

The objective function is:

$$\text{Minimize } P = M_{10} + M_{20} + M_{30} + M_{40} + M_{50} + M_{60} + M_{70} + 60x_{END}$$

The solution for this model is:

Total minimum project cost = 2,640

$$\begin{aligned}
x_{10} &= 0 & M_{10} &= 100 \\
x_{20} &= 0 & M_{20} &= 170 \\
x_{30} &= 5 & M_{30} &= 150 \\
x_{40} &= 3 & M_{40} &= 350 \\
x_{50} &= 3 & M_{50} &= 200 \\
x_{60} &= 8 & M_{60} &= 550 \\
x_{70} &= 14 & M70 &= 100 \\
x_{END} &= 17
\end{aligned}$$

∴ Project duration = 17 weeks

We can observe that only $M_{20}$ and $M_{40}$ in the result are different from their normal cost $U_{20}$ and $U_{40}$ respectively. By comparing $M_{20}$ and $U_{20}$, we can know that activity 20 is shortened by 1 week. Similarly, we can know that activity 40 is also shortened by 1 week. The normal (original) project duration is 19 weeks (see example 15.1) and the optimal project duration is found to be 17 weeks, because the two activities (20 and 40) are each shortened by 1 week.

Readers can compare the result with that given in Chapter 14.

# 16

# CONTRACTUAL CLAIMS USING CPM

## 1. Introduction

In running a construction contract, variations usually arise, particularly the variations of activity durations. Contractors are sometimes entitled to (and sometimes not of course) the extension of time of the contract period. In the dispute of extension of time between the employer (owner) and the contractor, a bar chart can never help settle the dispute. Instead, the critical path method must be used. The following case study will illustrate the point.

## 2. Case Study 1

Fig. 16.1 shows the main activities of a construction contract and their sequence.

**Legend :-**

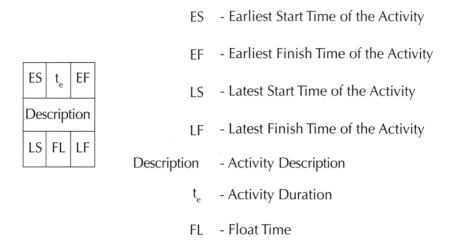

| ES | $t_e$ | EF |
|---|---|---|
| Description | | |
| LS | FL | LF |

ES  - Earliest Start Time of the Activity

EF  - Earliest Finish Time of the Activity

LS  - Latest Start Time of the Activity

LF  - Latest Finish Time of the Activity

Description  - Activity Description

$t_e$  - Activity Duration

FL  - Float Time

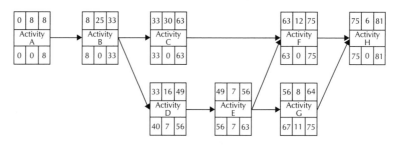

**Critical path: A-B-C-F-H**
**Project duration: 81 days**

**Fig. 16.1**  CPM network for a construction contract.

The critical path is A-B-C-F-H and the project duration is 81 days. This work programme was submitted by the contractor to the employer, through the engineering representative, as one of the contract documents when the contract was awarded.

During the construction of activity D, the contractor encountered unforeseen difficulties which were not expected under normal conditions. In order to overcome these difficulties, the time taken to complete this activity by the contractor was 30 days, not 16 days as originally shown in the contract programme.

At the time the contractor discovered the unexpected difficulties, he had commenced the activity 6 days after the earliest start time. The earliest start time of activity D, according to the original programme, was 33 days after the commencement of the project, but because he knew that the activity had 7 days of float, he took advantage of the float and started this activity on Day 39 (6 days later than the original planned earliest start Day 33).

So, the contractor recalculated the project completion date and it is shown in Fig. 16.2. The project duration became 94 days and the critical path was re-routed to A-B-D-E-F-H. Therefore, he claimed against the employer an extension of time of 13 days (i.e. 94 – 81 = 13).

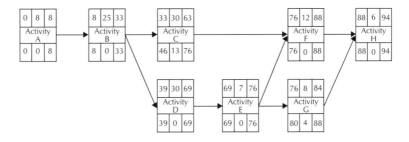

**Critical path: A-B-D-E-F-H**
**Project duration: 94 days**

**Fig. 16.2** Modified CPM network after activity D was delayed (contractor's view).

The employer, however, argued that the contractor should not count the 6 days float for activity D. If it was the case, the project duration should be 88 days, as shown in Fig. 16.3. Therefore, the employer agreed to give only 7 days (i.e. 88 – 81 = 7) of extension of time to the contractor.

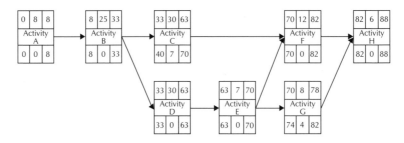

**Critical path: A-B-D-E-F-H**
**Project duration: 88 days**

**Fig. 16.3**  Modified CPM network after activity D was delayed
(employer's view).

The dispute was reviewed by the engineering representative, who, although employed by the owner (i.e. employer), should give impartial judgement because of his professional status. The engineering representative judged that because the difficulties were discovered after the 6 days float had been used, the float should belong to the contractor, and therefore the contractor was entitled to 13 days of extension of time.

However, if the case was not like this but a different one, that was, if the contractor could have anticipated the difficulties well before Day 33 (the earliest start time of activity D) and knew at a much earlier date that the activity would take 30 days instead of the original 16 days, then, in such a case, the contractor would be entitled to only 7 days of extension of time. The principle is: the float should belong to the employer if the contractor has not yet used the float. This is because in the conditions of contract used in Hong Kong, there is a clause saying that 'the Contractor shall commence the execution of the Works and shall proceed with diligence and expedition in regular progression or as may be directed by the superintending officer so that the whole of the Works shall be completed by the date for completion'.

Readers should note at this juncture that whenever an extension of time is granted, the CPM network and the programme of work have to be amended. So, there is a need to update the 'as-built programme' from time to time for the preparation of settling another new dispute.

After the above dispute had been settled, the engineering representative requested the contractor to propose a new method of construction for activity E because the owner suddenly required a higher quality of work on this activity. The contractor complied with the engineering representative's instruction, and he needed to take 15 days to carry out the work instead of 7 days. At the same time, the contractor obtained permission from the engineering representative to relax certain requirements for activity F, and would complete this work in 6 days instead of 12 days.

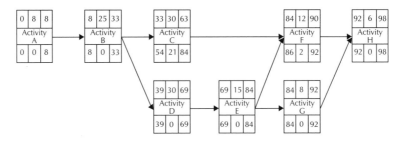

**Critical path: A-B-D-E-G-H**
**Project duration: 98 days**

**Fig. 16.4** Modified CPM network after the durations of activities D, E and F have been changed.

Due to such variations, the new project duration would be 98 days, and the critical path has been re-routed to A-B-D-E-G-H, as shown in Fig. 16.4. The engineering representative would grant the contractor an extension of 4 days (i.e. 98 -94 = 4) based on the critical path network. Readers now should be able to appreciate why it was said earlier that a bar chart can never be able to help settle disputes in connection with the extension of time in a construction contract and only CPM can do such a job.

## 3.    Case Study 2

We are going to use the same project network as used in Case Study 1 to illustrate further the settlement of contractual disputes.

Before the actual works commenced, the main contractor entered into a sub-contract with a direct subcontractor, who would carry out activity D, and another subcontract with a nominated subcontractor, who would carry out activity E. The main contractor at that time provided the engineering representative with the critical path programme as shown in Fig. 16.1, which is reproduced as Fig. 16.5 for easy reference. The programme was acceptable to the engineering representative. The subcontractors also had a review of the programme and then signed the subcontract agreements, which included a copy of the programme, without any objections. The main contractor then commenced work on the correct date.

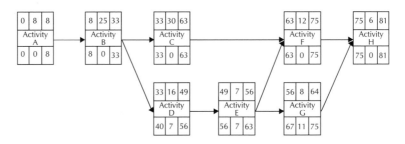

**Critical Path: A-B-C-F-H**
**Project duration: 81 days**

**Fig. 16.5**   CPM network for the construction contract.

When the work was in progress, the main contractor experienced some difficulties with his direct subcontractor who had insufficient labourers to carry out activity D. Hence, the 7 days float of this activity was used up. Then, the nominated subcontractor started working on activity E with no float. After commencing work, he soon found that the work (activity E) was much more complicated than he originally anticipated, and in any case, the 7 days activity duration written on the original programme was totally insufficient. He took 14 days instead of 7 days to complete this activity.

The main contractor hence revised the critical path programme and found that the project duration should be 88 days, as shown in Fig. 16.6, instead of 81 days as calculated originally.

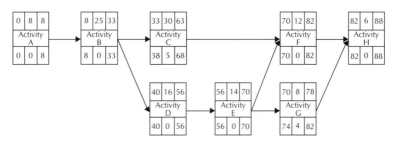

**Critical Path: A-B-D-E-F-H**
**Project duration: 88 days**

**Fig. 16.6** Modified CPM network after the float of activity D was used up by the direct subcontractor and activity E was delayed by the nominated subcontractor.

The main contractor wrote to the engineering representative, attaching the CPM programme calculations, to ask for an extension of time due to the reasons that he had the rights to use up the float of activity D and that the 7 days delay of Activity E was caused by the nominated subcontractor. The nominated subcontractor also wrote to the engineering representative (with a copy of the letter sent to the main contractor) claiming an extension of time arising from the delay caused by activity D using up the float time. He argued that if the work (activity E) had commenced 7 days earlier, there would have been no delay.

The engineering representative, after careful consideration, decided that there would be no extension of time and 7 days liquidated damages would be imposed to the main contractor if the latter failed to speed up the progress of the remaining activities to catch up with the original programme (81 days as agreed). The reasons were that there was no variation of the contract and that the fault (the delay) was not caused by the owner nor the engineering representative but by the contractor (or his subcontractors).

The main contractor was entitled to claim the said liquidated damages from the nominated subcontractor because the latter had agreed to the 7 days duration of activity E in the critical path programme, which formed a part of the contract, at the very beginning when the subcontract agreement was signed.

From the case study readers can see the important role the critical path method plays in helping to settle contractual disputes.

## Acknowledgement

*Acknowledgement is due to Mr Don R. Dalby, principal consultant of D&R Dalby, an Australian based contract administration services firm, for providing much valuable information for this chapter.*

# 17

# RESOURCE MANAGEMENT

## 1. Introduction

In Chapter 11, the float time of an activity was introduced. We saw how the float of an activity can be shown on a bar chart. From the bar chart, the relationship between the non-critical activities (with float) and the critical activities (without float) can be determined. In the processes of network analysis, however, we have not yet considered the availability of resources and the smoothness of the demand for labour for a particular project.

In this chapter, readers will see how the float time is used to optimize the resources allocation of a project.

## 2. The Resource Allocation Graph

The network illustrated in Chapter 12 is reproduced again in Fig. 17.1. We are going to see how resources can be allocated in such a way that level of demand for resources can be smoothened.

The critical path is: A-B-C-F-I-J-K and the project duration is 38 weeks.

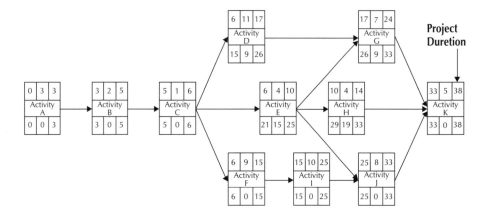

**Fig. 17.1** Network used in Chapter 12.

Suppose that the costs of completing the activities are estimated as given in Table 17.1.

| Activity | $t_e$ (weeks) | Cost per week | Total cost ($) |
|----------|---------------|---------------|----------------|
| A | 3 | 1,000 | 3,000 |
| B | 2 | 1,500 | 3,000 |
| C | 1 | 1,600 | 1,600 |
| D | 11 | 800 | 8,800 |
| E | 4 | 700 | 2,800 |
| F | 9 | 1,200 | 10,800 |
| G | 7 | 500 | 3,500 |
| H | 4 | 1,300 | 5,200 |
| I | 10 | 900 | 9,000 |
| J | 8 | 1,400 | 11,200 |
| K | 5 | 600 | 3,000 |

**Table 17.1** Durations of the project activities and the costs resources required.

Fig. 17.2 is a graph of resources in $/week for the critical activities against time (weeks). The graph is called a **histogram**.

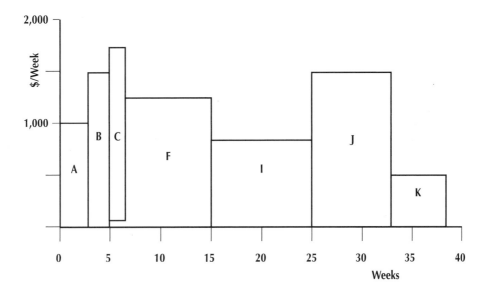

**Fig. 17.2** Histogram for the critical activities.

The cost of each critical activity is represented by the area of each rectangle in the histogram. The positions of the rectangles representing costs of critical activities in any way are fixed and cannot be altered. The non-critical activities, however, can be more flexible in this respect. If we set all the non-critical activities to start at their respective earliest start times, the histogram will be that in Fig. 17.3.

## 3. Optimizing Resource Allocation

Fig. 17.3 shows that for the first few weeks and the last few weeks, the resource utilized (in terms of money) is not more than $1,000 per week. However, during week 11 to week 14, it suddenly jumps to $3,300 per week. Certainly, such a situation is not desirable. It is better to have a more evenly distributed resource utilization throughout the project.

We do this only visually here. If we adjust the start times of the non-critical activities within their allowable float times, the histogram will be smoothened.

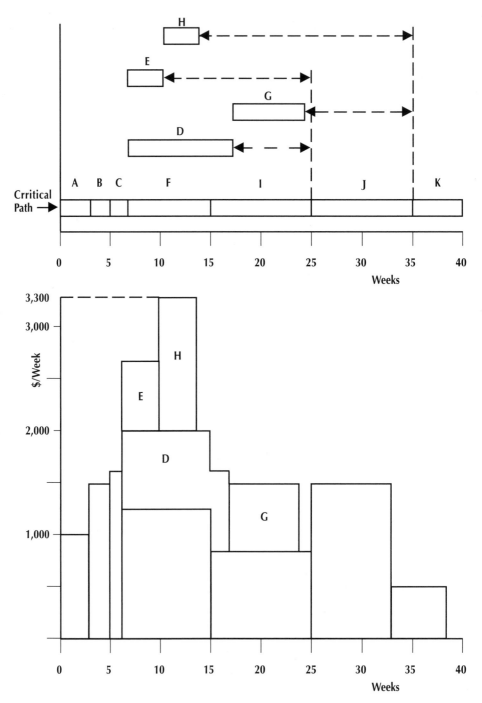

**Fig. 17.3** Bar chart (above) and histogram (below) for the project (all activities start at earliest start times).

Fig. 17.4 shows how the non-critical activities have been adjusted.

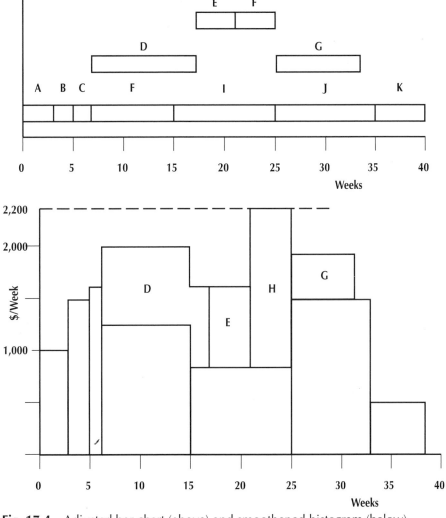

**Fig. 17.4** Adjusted bar chart (above) and smoothened histogram (below).

The maximum total resource required is only $2,200 per week.

The above smoothening process is done by visual checking only. Although the start times of the non-critical activities have been adjusted, their basic logic (or sequence) defined in the network must not be disturbed. In other words, Activity D can commence only after Activity C is completed and must finish before Activity G commences; Activity G can commence only after Activities D and E are completed and must finish before Activity K commences and so on.

## 4.    **Worked Example**

Fig. 17.5 shows a network diagram for a construction project and Table 17.2 gives the respective durations and resources required of the activities.

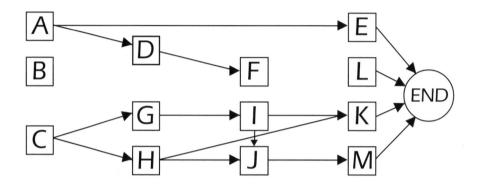

**Fig. 17.5**    Network diagram for a project.

| Activity | Description (weeks) | Resource per week |
|---|---|---|
| A | 3 | 2 |
| B | 6 | 3 |
| C | 4 | 3 |
| D | 2 | 2 |
| E | 5 | 4 |
| F | 1 | 2 |
| G | 3 | 2 |
| H | 4 | 3 |
| I | 2 | 4 |
| J | 4 | 2 |
| K | 8 | 3 |
| L | 7 | 2 |
| M | 3 | 3 |

**Table 17.2**    Durations of the project activities and resources required.

The resource element represents the number of carpenters required per week for the completion of each activity in the duration shown. Determine a contract programme which allows a smooth increase and then decrease in the number of carpenters. Show the consequent weekly requirement for carpenters in the form of a histogram.

Solution

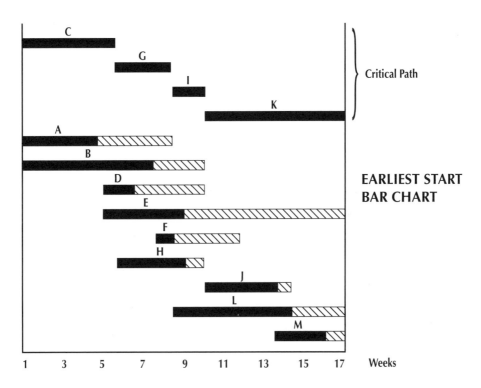

The above bar chart is drawn based on all activities commencing at the earlist start time. The commencement of the non-critical activities can be adjusted within their floats so that the histogram becomes levelled. This is shown in Fig. 17.6.

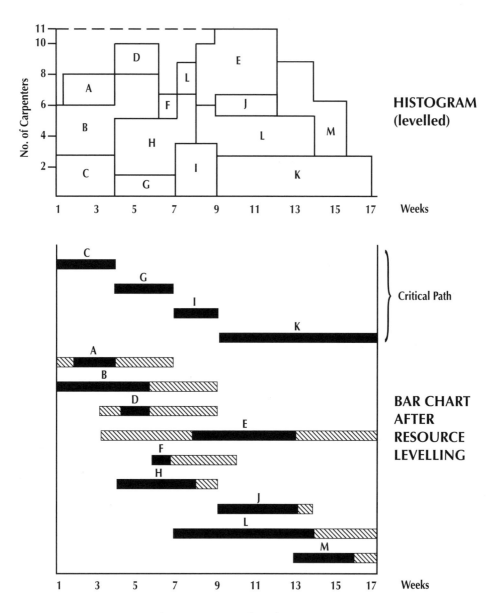

**Fig.17.6**   Example solution.

## 5.    Resource Management in Practice

In this chapter, we have discussed the basic principles of resource optimization, which is just a small part of resource management. Resource management is a much more complicated exercise in real practice.

Normally, the duration and resource requirement of an activity are estimated based on what is normally needed. If the time duration of an activity has to be reduced and is made shorter than is normally required, the resource requirement will be higher than normal, as discussed in Chapter 14. The two examples given in this chapter are much over-simplified because the durations of the activities and their respective resource requirements have been assumed to be fixed (at normal conditions). In actual practice, however, they can be shortened or lengthened in order to cope with the resources available. In doing so, the project duration will be changed and the resource requirement will be different from what has been originally estimated. Resource management can become very complicated if all these variables are considered.

In practice, resource management is further complicated for the following reasons:

1.  A considerable number of different resources (not only carpenter or manpower, as illustrated in the worked example) must be considered at the same time. Labour, plant and material are the most basic resources. Labour alone is further divided into many different trades. The same applies to plant and material. It is not unusual to have nearly a hundred resources (or even more) that have to be considered for a single project.
2.  It is a common practice that the resources available have to be shared between more than one project. This makes resource management even more complicated.
3.  The limitation on the availability of certain types of resources may cause a change in the sequence of the activities of the critical path network. For example, Activities C and D (as defined in Table 10.2 of Chapter 10) can be done simultaneously if available manpower is unlimited, but because of manpower limitation, Activity D may have to be carried out after Activity C is completed, or vice versa. Therefore, repeated revisions of the sequence of the activities of the network are necessary in the process of resource allocation exercises. This will be further illustrated in the next section.

## 6.   Resource Levelling Using Computer Software

There are many popular software packages available in the market for critical path analysis (see Chapter 18 also). Nearly all of them have resource levelling functions. A brief description of these functions is given below.

Look at a very simple network consisting of three activities as shown in Fig. 17.7.

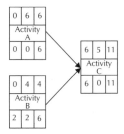

**Fig. 17.7**   The network of a simple project consisting of 3 activities.

The  project can be represented by the bar chart as shown in Fig. 17.8.

| Activity | Days | | |
|---|---|---|---|
| | 5 | 10 | 15 |
| A | | | |
| B | | | |
| C | | | |

**Fig. 17.8**   Project bar chart.

The project duration is 11 days. The project can be completed with such a duration only if there is no resource constraints. However, if  both Activties A and B require a concreting gang but only one concrete gang is allocated for this project, then, because of the resource constraint, the project duration becomes longer (15 days) and the bar chart will become either Fig. 17.9 or Fig. 17.10.

| Activity | Days | | |
|---|---|---|---|
| | 5 | 10 | 15 |
| A | | | |
| B | | | |
| C | | | |

**Fig. 17.9**   Bar chart due to resource constraint (Case 1).

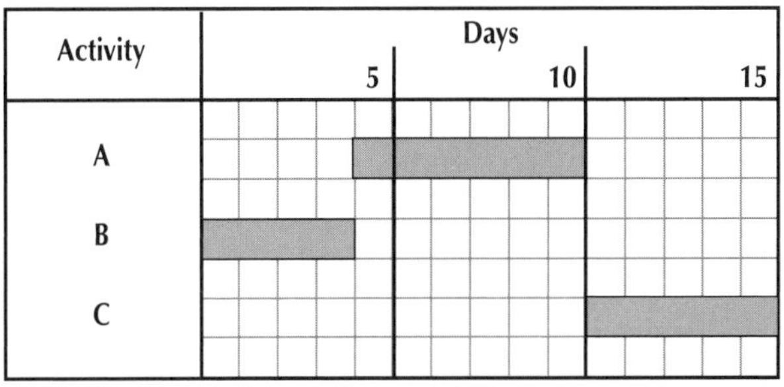

**Fig. 17.10**   Bar chart due to resource constraint (Case 2).

Which bar chart is better, Fig. 17.9 or Fig. 17.10?  The answer is that one can have one's own choice of the bar chart by defining one's own priority.

For example, if the 'longest activity duration' is the priority, the choice will be the bar chart in Fig. 17.9, because Activity A has a longer duration than Activity B. However, if the 'largest float' is the priority, then the choice is the bar chart in Fig. 17.10, because Activity B's float is larger than Activty A's float (floats for Activities A and B are 0 and 2 respectively). If the 'least float' is the priority, the result is the same bar chart as  the 'longest activity durtion' case, that is, Fig. 17.9.

This is how the common CPM computer software packages available in the market work in resource levelling. When a priority is made known to the computer, it will generate a bar chart according to the priority defined. These computer software packages usually analyse the project network at the beginning and gives the user a bar chart with the shortest possible project duration by assuming that there are no resource constraints. The user can then input the available resources into the computer if the user wants to use the resource levelling function of the software. If there are limited resources to be shared by more than one activity, the project duration will become longer and the arrangement of the activities will be changed (originally in parallel but now in series), as is explained in the above example. The new arrangement of activities depends on how the priority is defined by the user.

For some CPM computer packages, such as **Primavera**, a user can define more than one priority. The software allows the user to enter a number of priorities in the order of decreasing importance. Lower priorities will not be satisfed at the expense of higher priorities. The software is able to automatically generate a work programme (or bar chart) which will have no resource conflicts, and at the same time, the project will be completed at its shortest possible duration, although this duration is longer than the one calculated earlier when no resource constraints were assumed. Other computer packages, such as **MS Project** and **Time-Line**, on the other hand, do not allow the user to define any priorities and the packages have already had build-in priorities. They will use their own build-in priorities to carry out resource levelling.

# 18

# COMMON
# PROGRAMMING
# SOFTWARE

A number of computer packages for planning and programming are available in the market place. A brief introduction of these packages is given below.

## 1.    Powerproject Teamplan

Powerproject Teamplan (http://www.astadev.com) addresses real-time programming and resource management issues across the company. It can help manage all projects, resources and costs, and is a scalable solution suitable for individual, departmental and enterprise level planning.

It is an easy-to-use software application that helps reduce costs, meet deadlines and speed up completion dates in the house building business.

The software is popular because it:

*   is easy to use
*   provides total visibility across all projects
*   plans resource requirements accurately
*   speeds up completion rates
*   keeps people informed

- is supported by people who know the industry
- is used by leading house builders, both large and small

## 2. Planview

Planview (http://www.planview.com/planview.html) is used to plan work and workforce, manage the complexity of contracts, budgets, resource pools, projects, service departments, risks and changes. The staff, contractors, time and expenses status can be tracked to improve management skills and to drive billings. This software has been proven at many Fortune 1000 and Global 500 companies and other leading organizations worldwide.

'Manage Work' is the scheduling tool in Planview for both projects and service work. Resource and projects managers can use this software to view, filter and sort work and resources. Planview can help check the resource availability — projects, recurring work, service and administrative before finalizing the schedules.

### 2.1 Query and Grouping Features

Manage Work is designed for scheduling, assigning resources, authorizing resources to service work and tracking project progress. It uses the powerful and flexible structures of the repository to filter and display information. These structures support automatic workflow, such as re-adjusting responsibility when the work status changes. Planview's web-based collaboration then notifies the appropriate managers of the change in work or resource availability. Work can be grouped by work breakdown structure, customer, work type, location, or any additional hierarchical structures or attributes. Resources can be grouped by organization breakdown structure, skill/role, grade, location or additional hierarchical structures or attributes. Structures can be shared between work and resources and can include multiple entries such as skill sets. Using these features, information can be displayed by department, customer, skills required, current status or a variety of other techniques that one might define, for a management view or a detailed view.

### 2.2 Interactive Gantts With Profiles

Planview has the first interactive Web Gantt. The users have accessed to Work Detail, Find Qualified Resources and Assign Resources. Once an activity has been scheduled, the schedule bars can be moved with the drag and drop functionality, or they can be re-sized to change dates and/or durations. Milestones can also be viewed and moved from within the Gantt View.

## 2.3   Planview's Collaborative CPA

Planview enterprise planning, collaboration and scheduling functions are executed on the server and based on organization-wide workforce availability and schedules. Having the enterprise planning engines process on the application server provides a functionality never before available. The engines hold a 'schedule data model' in memory, so schedule changes that impact other departments or other projects are identified and notification is automatically sent to the appropriate managers. Planview's collaborative CPA (critical path analysis) alerts managers of changes in schedules, and allows the managers the final decision to revise their resource schedules.

## 3.   Primavera

Primavera Project Planner (http://www.primavera.com/products/index/html) is a choice for high-performance project management software. It is designed to handle large-scale, highly sophisticated and multifaceted projects. This software is able to organize projects with up to 100,000 activities and provides unlimited resources and an unlimited number of target plans. It offers a single database solution that provides simultaneous access to project files by multiple users throughout the project. Web features also make it easy to keep the whole team informed.

The software offers impressive capability for integrating its data with information throughout the organization. It supports a wide variety of data exchange formats. The user can cut and paste with other Windows applications, or use Object Linking and Embedding to link information from other applications.

## 4.   Microsoft Project

Microsoft Project (http://www.microsoft.com/office/project/default.asp) provides knowledge workers with the flexibility to plan collaboratively and track projects and deliver the results according to business demands. Introduced to work closely with Microsoft Project, a new companion product, Microsoft Project Central, is a web-based collaboration tool allowing two-way communication between everyone involved in a project and also allowing data access to anyone, even without Microsoft Project on their desktops.

The benefits of Microsoft Project are its ability to:

- Improve team productivity by involving team members and other stakeholders in project management
- Increase the usefulness of Microsoft Project data for users
- Extend project management across the organization

## 4.1    New Features

### Personal Gantt chart

This renders Gantt views such as those in Microsoft Project to outline each team member's own tasks across multiple projects.

### New task

Team members can create tasks; the project manager can approve those new tasks before adding them to the project plan.

### Task delegation

Once assigned by the project manager, tasks may be delegated from leads to team members or form peer to peer. Delegation can be disabled.

## 4.2    Improved Features

### Scaling and printing

Users can print documents more efficiently and easily with new printing and scaling options and improved behaviour of existing options.

### Workgroup

Project managers can assign task responsibilities and track project status across workgroups to keep the project on track. Users can use email alone, or with Microsoft Project Central, they can exchange project information at a web site on their intranet or the internet.

### Timesheet

This is where team members can see their assignments across projects, enter updates and easily send them to the project manager.

# BIBLIOGRAPHY

Abdul-Rahman, H. 1995. 'The cost of non-conformance during a highway project: A case study', *Construction Management and Economics*, 3, pp. 23-32.

Ahmed, S.M. et al. 1998. 'Implementing and maintaining a quality assurance system - A case study of a Hong Kong construction contractor', *Proceedings of the Third International Conference on ISO 9000 & Total Quality Management*, Hong Kong Baptist University, pp. 450-456.

Ahuja, H.N.,S.P. Dozzi and S.M. Abourizk. 1994. *Project Management: Techniques in Planning and Controlling Construction Projects*, 2nd Edition. New York: John Wiley.

Ashford, J.L. 1989. *The Management of Quality in Construction*. London: E & FN Spon.

Burati, J.L. 1990. *Total Quality Management: The Competitive Edge*. Publication 10-4, Construction Industry Institute, Austin, Texas.

Burati, J.L., M.F. Mathews and S.N. Kalidindi. 1992. 'Quality management organisation and techniques', *Journal of Construction Engineering and Management*, Vol. 118, No.1, Mar 1992, pp. 112-128.

Byrne, M.J. 1993. 'Quality initiatives in public works', Quality Management Policies for Civil and Construction Contracts by the Hong Kong Polytechnic Quality and Reliability Centre, pp. 45-56.

Chartered Institute of Building. 1983. *Code of Estimating Practice.*

European Construction Institute. 1993. 'Total quality in construction', Stage 2 Report of the Total Quality Management Task Force, April 1993.

Fan, L. and B. Loader. 1991. 'Quality assurance and the construction industry', *Shui On Construction Review,* 1991, pp. 38-48.

Gould, F.E. and N.E. Joyce. 2002. *Construction Project Management,* Professional Edition. New Jersey: Prentice-Hall.

Haltenhoff, C.E. 1999. *The CM Contracting System: Fundamentals and Practices.* New Jersey: Prentice Hall.

Harris, F. and R. McCaffer. 2001. *Modern Construction Management,* 5th Edition. Oxford: Blackwell Science.

Hellard, R.B. 1993. *Total Quality in Construction Projects - Achieving Profitability With Customer Satisfaction.* London: Thomas Telford.

Hong Kong Government. 1992. *General Conditions of Contract for the Airport Core Programme Civil Engineering Works.*

Hong Kong Government. 1999. *General Conditions of Contract for Civil Engineering Works.*

Hong Kong Government. 1999. *General Conditions of Contract for Design and Build Contracts.*

Hong Kong Quality Assurance Agency. 1996. *Buyer's Guide.*

International Labour Office. 1995. *Social and Labour Issues Concerning Migrant Workers in the Construction Industry,* International Labour Office, Geneva.

Kam, C.W. and S.L. Tang. 1998. 'ISO 9000 for building and civil engineering contractors', *Transactions of Hong Kong Institution of Engineers,* Vol. 5, No.2, pp. 6-10.

Kam, C.W. and S.L. Tang. 1995. 'A comparison of the 1987 and 1994 editions', *The Asia Engineer,* March 1995, pp. 10-14.

Kam, C.W. and S.L. Tang. 1997. 'Development and implementation of quality assurance in public construction works in Singapore and Hong Kong', *International Journal of Quality and Reliability Management,* Vol. 14, No.9, pp. 909-928.

Kubal, M.T. 1994. *Engineered Quality in Construction — Partnering and TQM.* New York: McGraw-Hill.

Labour Department. 1999. *Report of the Commissioner for Labour 1999.* Hong Kong Government.

Lam, S.W., C.M. Low and W.A. Teng. 1994. *ISO 9000 in Construction.* New York: McGraw-Hill.

McCaffer, R. and A.N. Baldwin. 1984. *Estimating and Tendering for Civil Engineering Works.* London: Granada.

Oakland, J.S. 1993. *Total Quality Management.* Oxford: Butterworth-Heinemann.

Oberlender, G.D. 2000. *Project Management for Engineering and Construction,* 2nd Edition. New York: McGraw-Hill.

Poon, S.W. and Y.Q. Xu. 1997. 'Problems of small Chinese contractors in Hong Kong during quality assurance system implementation', *Proceedings of International Conference on Leadership and Total Quality Management in Construction and Building,* 6-8 October 1997, Singapore, pp. 183-188.

Rowlinson, S. 1997. *Hong Kong Construction — Site Safety Management.* Hong Kong: Sweet & Maxwell.

Rowlinson, S.W. and A. Walker. 1995. *The Construction Industry in Hong Kong.* Hong Kong: Longman.

Safety Specialist Group. 1997. 'The Hong Kong engineers — Engineering for public safety', *Proceedings of the HKIE Safety Conference 1997,* Hong Kong Institution of Engineers.

Shammsa-Toma, M., D.E. Seumour and L.Clark. 1996. 'The effectiveness of formal quality management systems in achieving the required cover in reinforced concrete', *Construction Management and Economics,* 14, pp. 353-364.

Stebbing, L.1989. *Quality Assurance: The Route to Efficiency and Competitiveness.* Chicester, England: Ellis Horwood.

Tam, C.M. 1996. 'Benefits and costs of the implementation of ISO 9000 in the construction industry of Hong Kong', *Journal of Real Estate and Construction,* 6, pp.53-66.

Tang, S.L. 1999. *Linear Optimization in Applications.* Hong Kong: Hong Kong University Press.

Tang, S.L. and C.W. Kam. 1999. 'A survey of ISO 9001 implementation in engineering consultants in Hong Kong', *International Journal of Quality and Reliability Management,* Vo. 16, Nos. 6 & 7, pp. 562-574.

Tang, S.L. and S.W. Poon. 1987. *Project Management, Volume 1*. The Hong Kong Polytechnic.

Tang, S.L., and S.W. Poon. 1987. *Project Management, Volume 2*. The Hong Kong Polytechnic.

Tang, S.L., S.W. Poon, C.H. Li and C.S. Chung.1996. *Management Practice of Large Constructing Firm in Hong Kong,* Research Report, Department of Civil and Structural Engineering, The Hong Kong Polytechnic University.

Tingey, M.O. 1997. *Comparing ISO 9000, Malcolm Baldrige, and the SEICMM for Software: A Reference and Selection Guide.* New Jersey: Prentice Hall.

Wong, C.K. 1994. Study of Tendering on Airport Core Programme Projects. BEng Final Year Project, The Hong Kong Polytechnic University.

Wong, K.W. 1987. *A Study on the Safety of Hand-dug Caisson Construction in Hong Kong.* The Hong Kong Polytechnic.

Wong, K.W. and C.M. Cheung. 1996. 'Construction Safety Management in Hong Kong', *Proceedings of the First International Conference of CIB Working Commission W99,* Lisbon, Portugal, pp. 243-249.

# ABOUT
# THE
# AUTHORS

---

**S. L. TANG**

B.Sc.(Eng), M.Sc., Ph.D., MHKIE, MICE, MCIWEM

S. L. Tang is a faculty member in the Department of Civil and Structural Engineering of the Hong Kong Polytechnic University. He is a Chartered Civil Engineer and obtained his B.Sc. in Civil Engineering from the University of Hong Kong, M.Sc. in Construction Engineering from the University of Singapore, and Ph.D. from the Civil Engineering Department of Loughborough University of Technology, U.K. Dr Tang had about seven years of working experience in civil engineering practice with contracting/ consulting firms and government departments before he joined the Hong Kong Polytechnic University. He is currently involved in the teaching and research of construction management and has written over 80 journal/ conference papers and books related to the areas of his expertise.

## S. W. POON

M.Sc., Ph.D., C.Eng., MHKIE, RPE, MIStructE, MCIWEM

S. W. Poon is a faculty member in the Department of Real Estate and Construction at the University of Hong Kong. Before joining the department, he taught at the National University of Singapore and the Hong Kong Polytechnic University. He is a Chartered Structural Engineer and a Corporate Member of the Hong Kong Institution of Engineers. He obtained his M.Sc. in Construction and Ph.D. from Loughborough University, U.K. Dr Poon was the Chairman (2000/2001) of the Safety Specialist Group of the Hong Kong Institution of Engineers and is a Senior Member of Professional Committee of Construction Safety, the China Association of Construction Industry. His research interests include construction and project management, temporary works design and construction, and failures during construction. He is a co-author of a self-study package of Project Management published by the Hong Kong Polytechnic University.

## Syed M. AHMED

B.Sc.(Eng), M.Sc.(Eng), Ph.D., P.E., M.ASCE

Syed Mahmood Ahmed is a faculty member in the Department of Construction Management at the Florida International University (FIU) in Miami. Before joining FIU, Dr Ahmed was an academic staff member in the Department of Civil and Structural Engineering of the Hong Kong Polytechnic University from 1995 to 1999. He obtained his B.Sc. in Civil Engineering from the University of Engineering & Technology, Lahore, Pakistan in 1984. After working in the private and public sectors for over three years, he joined the Georgia Institute of Technology, Atlanta, USA in 1987, from where he completed his M.Sc. in Civil Engineering in 1989 and his Ph.D. in 1993. During his doctoral studies, he also worked for CRSS, a top construction management firm in Atlanta for a number of years. After completing his Ph.D. he returned to Pakistan where he worked as an Assistant Director (Special Project Directorate) in the Capital Development Authority (CDA) in Islamabad before taking up an academic career. Dr Ahmed has over 50 publications in refereed international journals and conferences. He is a registered professional engineer, member of the American Society of Civil Engineer and member of the UNESCO International Centre for Engineering Education.

## Francis K. W. WONG

B.Sc.(Hons), M.Sc., Ph.D., FCIOB, FHKIE, FHKICM, RPE(Bldg.), MCIArb, MIM, MIOSH

Francis Wong is the Associate Head of the Department of Building and Real Estate of the Hong Kong Polytechnic University. After obtaining a B.Sc. (Hons) degree in Building from Brighton Polytechnic in the U.K., he returned to Hong Kong in 1980 to work for a building contractor, and the Mass Transit Railway Corporation two years later. In 1984, he joined the Hong Kong Polytechnic. In 1988, he completed his Master's degree at the University of London, majoring in building economics and management. He obtained his Ph.D. with the topic of 'Construction Safety in Hong Kong' from South Bank University in 2000. He is a Fellow Member of the Hong Kong Institution of Engineers (HKIE), a Founding Member as well as the Chairman (1999/2000) of the Safety Specialist Group (SSG) of HKIE. Dr Wong is currently the HKIE Representative to sit on the Construction Industry Safety and Health Committee of the Occupational Safety and Health Council from 2001 to 2004. He is a Fellow Member of the Chartered Institute of Building (CIOB), and was the Senior Vice-Chairman of the CIOB (Hong Kong Branch) in year 1994/95. He is also a Fellow and a Founding Member of the Hong Kong Institute of Construction Managers.